Behind Tax Policy Controversies

Behind Tax Policy Controversies

Social, Legal and
Economic Foundations

Steven M. Sheffrin
Tulane University

ANTHEM PRESS

Anthem Press
An imprint of Wimbledon Publishing Company
www.anthempress.com

This edition first published in UK and USA 2023
by ANTHEM PRESS
75–76 Blackfriars Road, London SE1 8HA, UK
or PO Box 9779, London SW19 7ZG, UK
and
244 Madison Ave #116, New York, NY 10016, USA

© 2023 Steven M. Sheffrin

The author asserts the moral right to be identified as the author of this work.

British Library Cataloguing-in-Publication Data
A catalogue record for this book is available from the British Library.

Library of Congress Control Number: 2023900040
A catalog record for this book has been requested.

ISBN-13: 978-1-83998-491-4 (Hbk)
ISBN-10: 1-83998-491-0 (Hbk)

ISBN-13: 978-1-83998-494-5 (Pbk)
ISBN-10: 1-83998-494-5 (Pbk)

This title is also available as an e-book.

to
Rujun

CONTENTS

LIST OF TABLES

PREFACE

Sometimes I am asked why I find writing and thinking about taxes so fascinating. After all, most people associate taxes with unpleasant thoughts: the annual chore of filing income taxes, sales taxes adding unwelcome costs to our major purchases, and the repetitive political debates about whether the tax system is fair. I respond by saying that to understand taxes you need to understand all the competing tensions in our daily life—tax is a window on our society.

This book is designed to be a short, critical introduction to the controversies in tax policy. The main thesis of the book is that there is a deeper substructure to debates about tax policy that underlie many of the controversies. By understanding the nature of this substructure one can place the debates about tax policy into a broader perspective. The chapters in the book elucidate this underlying architecture drawing on ideas from economics, law, philosophy, psychology, and political science. By drawing on perspectives from social science, we hope to go beyond Justice Benjamin Cardozo's admonition in the Supreme Court case *Welch v. Helvering* that tax controversies must be resolved by considering "life in all its fullness."[1]

Economic principles shape some of the foundations for the debates, particularly about the question of whether income taxes should be structured with a broad base and low rates, and whether the appropriate base of taxation should be consumption or income. Legal and administrative issues provide another foundation for tax policy, as certain structural features of the tax system—the separate existence of corporations, what is known as the realization principle for income taxation, and pure technical limits in administering the tax code—constrain the set of feasible tax policies. Legal perspectives also illuminate controversies about the meaning of potential disparate impacts of the tax code. To understand tax fairness, one must delve into philosophy and psychology. A key debate is whether we view taxation just through a purely distributional lens (who gets what) or whether we think about notions of process and deservingness to make sense of debates on tax fairness.

The book uses these tools to shed light on these issues, as well as on current debates. These include the appropriate goals for tax reform, the most judicious way to tax multinational corporations, our ability to tax the very wealthy, and whether the tax system has a racial subtext that must be addressed. It provides a succinct critical introduction to the key tax policy debates.

My goal in the book is to take readers to the frontiers of debates about tax policy without having to become an expert in law, economics, or philosophy. In undertaking this task, I have been fortunate to have the opportunity to refine this approach through teaching several interdisciplinary classes at Tulane University in both the Political Economy program of the Murphy Institute and the School of Law. The students in all these classes posed challenging questions, pointed me in new directions, and helped me refine and clarify the arguments.

Several my colleagues at Tulane provided valuable feedback on my work. First and foremost, James Alm of Economics and Kathleen Weaver of the Murphy Institute read all the first drafts of the chapters and provided incisive comments both on content and style. They also provided valuable encouragement along the way. I also received valuable insights from my colleagues in law, Adam Feibelman, Ann Lipton, and Stacy Seicshnaydre. I benefitted immensely over the years from the lively interdisciplinary atmosphere at Tulane and its Murphy Institute, where I had the opportunity to engage scholars from all disciplines. Four anonymous reviewers for Anthem Press provided fruitful suggestions which made their way into the final manuscript. I am indebted to all my colleagues and reviewers for their assistance in this project.

Note

1 Justice Cardozo was writing about whether certain expenses could be takes as immediate deductions against income. His full quote was "The standard set up by the statute is not a rule of law; rather it is a way of life. Life in all its fullness must supply the answer to the riddle." *Welch v. Helvering.* 290 U.S. 111.

Chapter 1

WHAT ARE TAX POLICY CONTROVERSIES ABOUT?

Taxes are part of the fabric of daily life, and the typical person has extensive experience with a variety of taxes, ranging from personal income to sales to property taxes. While the intricacies of taxes are certainly too arcane for most people to understand, there is a general belief that the average citizen has a basic understanding of the types of taxes they pay and accompanying opinions about the level and fairness of taxation.

The most common view—articulated routinely in the press—is that debates about taxes are really debates about "who pays what" or what parties bear the burden of financing our collective life. According to this view, most disputes about taxation can be reduced to finding out which parties bear the burden of taxes. Especially when it comes to time for debate on new tax proposals or to judge our politicians, we do focus on the relative burden of taxes. President Joe Biden, for example, campaigned in 2020 on a platform not to raise taxes on those making less than $400,000 in yearly income. This was reassuring to most taxpayers who believed they would not be affected by his proposals. This promise did constrain the type of taxes that could be considered, for example, ruling out gasoline taxes. Nonetheless, the focus during the presidential campaign and early governing period was on who would pay for the cost of his programs.

This common view—who pays what—unfortunately, presents an incomplete picture of tax controversies. It has two basic problems: first, it sweeps aside the social, political and psychological perspectives on taxes that are so important to the daily functioning of our tax system. The passions that taxes provoke—property tax revolts, outrage against arbitrary actions of the tax authorities, scorn and disdain for apparent tax evaders and scofflaws and the commonplace willingness to admire (and minimally tax) the large fortunes of the wealthy—can only be explained by a variety of social factors.[1]

The second and more profound problem with the common view is that it ignores the deeper root causes of many of the most important debates about taxation. Our periodic eruptions over tax fairness and tax burdens are like the occasional earthquake, with seismic eruptions triggered by underlying movements in tectonic plates.

This book is primarily about the tectonic plates—the deep understructure of controversies about taxation. The main thesis of the book is that there is a deep substructure to debates about tax policy that underlies many of the active and ongoing controversies. By understanding the nature of this substructure, one can place the debates about tax policy into a broader perspective. This book elucidates the underlying architecture drawing on important and essential ideas from economics, law, philosophy, psychology and political science.

In the process of elucidating the substructure of tax policy, I also provide a survey of the key issues that have emerged in tax policy, some traditional and some quite recent. Most tax policy issues do not have simple answers, so understanding the foundations of tax policy will enable the reader to better assess the underlying factors driving the key controversies.

What constitutes the architecture for tax policy? From economics, I draw on not only the basic idea of efficiency but also the notions of excess burden, the costs of taxation over and above the revenue that is raised and incidence, the analysis of who really bears the economic burden of a tax. From the study of tax law, I incorporate the complexities that arise from the need to respect formal legal structures—such as the independent legal status of corporations—while at the same time recognizing the true economic substance of transactions. Law also provides needed grounding—it encompasses the need for tax laws to be administrable and consistent with underlying business practices. I look to philosophy to provide a reasoned and disciplined discussion of perspectives on justice and fairness, while psychology can inform us whether those notions accord with human experience. Political science provides a concrete link between political ideals and actual outcomes for taxation through its careful empirical analysis.

Surface Eruptions

Before turning to the slow-moving tectonic plates, it will be useful to start in this introductory chapter by emphasizing a few of the surface eruptions, the social and political contexts of taxation. Here are a few striking examples to illustrate the importance of political, social and psychological factors in taxation.

- Most Americans associate the Boston Tea Party with the phrase "no taxation without representation" signifying that sovereignty and popular will must be closely tied to taxation. But the actual history and origin of the Boston Tea Party—when on December 16, 1773, American colonists dressed as Native Americans dumped tea into Boston Harbor—are more complex and contested. The proximate cause of the tea party was not an increase in British taxes on tea. In fact, it was the opposite.[2] The British Parliament took action to relieve financial pressures on the East Indian Tea Company by allowing them to export tea to the U.S. colonies without paying export duties. As a result, prices for the East Indian tea fell below the prices of Dutch tea which, in turn, undercut the profitable smuggling operations of Samuel Adams and John Hancock. Rather than a populist revolt, the Boston Tea Party was a struggle over market share. Prominent colonists such as George Washington and Benjamin Franklin opposed the actions of the colonists in Boston Harbor.

- The estate and gift tax in the United States is the most progressive of all federal taxes. Despite some changes in the limits over the years, typically only 0.1 percent of people who die each year will pay the estate tax.[3] Yet, public opinion polling ever since 1935 consistently shows that approximately 50 percent of survey respondents supports total repeal of the estate and gift tax.[4] It was abolished in the United States for one year in 2010. Some tax scholars believe that the pro-repeal poll responses can be attributed to ignorance about who pays the tax. But a more nuanced view suggests that the estate and gift tax—or "death tax"—touches on some fundamental aspect of American beliefs and life.[5] Other ostensibly progressive countries, such as Australia and Canada, do not have an estate or inheritance tax (although capital gains on assets are due at death). A story of "who gets what" does not fit the politics and public opinion associated with this tax.

- There are some circumstances where businesses seek out the privilege to pay tax. Owners of legal brothels in Nevada pay local business taxes but no state-level business taxes or sales taxes. They have consistently sought to be taxed by the state. The state has consistently refused to tax them. The reason is the legitimacy conferred by taxation. As Kitty Richards discusses, this is an instance of "expressive theory" in law applied to taxation. A Reno Gazette editorial is explicit on this point: "for the brothel industry, it's not about the money. Rather it's about the legitimacy that comes with being involved in a state-recognized taxpaying business."[6] In this case, taxes would have conferred a sense of normality and ordinariness to a business that was viewed with disdain by the majority of the legislature. Other examples of expressive taxation that Richards highlights include controversies about marriage penalties or bonuses and the denial of charitable status to organizations that discriminate based on race. In general, expressive theory emphasizes that taxes can convey social meaning.

- Tax revolts and protests provide another illustration of the social context of taxation. Miners in Kalgoorlie, Western Australia, led a major protest against the Australian Tax Office (ATO). During the 1980s and early 1990s, the miners came into newfound wealth and were lured by promoters to invest in borderline tax shelters. Many years later, the ATO decided these tax shelters were illegal and tried to assess back penalties and interest. As scholars have shown, the delay and abrupt nature of the change in the position of the tax authorities was what triggered a major tax revolt. Eventually, the miners would pay the back taxes (without the penalties and interest), so it was not the taxes that were at issue but the way they were mistreated through the process.[7] In the United States, the late 1990s witnessed protests against overzealous behavior by the Internal Revenue Service (IRS). Congressional hearings were held where IRS whistleblowers spoke from behind black screens with their voices altered to protect their identities. The eventual result was the passage of the Internal Revenue Structuring and Reform Act of 1998 which brought on, at least temporarily, a new "kinder and gentler" customer-oriented IRS.

As these episodes attest, many tax controversies do not directly involve questions about the distribution of tax burdens.

Other major controversies do eventually touch on tax burdens, but even those are rarely straightforward. As I demonstrate in this book, many of the debates about tax burdens rest on more fundamental bases.

Below the Surface

Here are three iconic examples that illustrate the need to go beyond the surface of tax controversies.

Billionaire taxation

Consider the taxes paid by billionaire Warren Buffett. In a 2007 interview, Warren Buffett revealed that he paid a lower tax rate on his income than his employees.[8] He asserted that he paid a tax rate of 17.7 percent, while the average for the employees he surveyed was 32.9 percent. Famously, Buffett also claimed he paid a lower rate than his secretary. These differences in tax rates may have shocked the average American but were unsurprising to anyone familiar with tax policy. Buffett earned most of his income from capital gains and dividends, while his employees earned their income from wages. Since tax rates on capital gains and dividends are lower than those on wages, the average tax rate for his employees would naturally be less than his. Of course, with his higher income, he would pay more in total taxes but do so at a lower rate.

President Barack Obama used Buffett's example to propose the Buffett Rule, a complex scheme that would effectively enforce a minimum tax rate of 30 percent for taxpayers whose income exceeded $1 million.[9] Despite its populist appeal, it was estimated to raise only $5 billion per year. The Buffett rule was never enacted into law.

A closer examination of Buffett's tax situation is more alarming. In 2021, ProPublica obtained 15 years of confidential tax return information for the top billionaires in the United States—either from an IRS employee or perhaps a hack of the IRS computer system.[10] ProPublica calculated tax rates for these billionaires, but not in the same way we normally calculate tax rates. Instead, they looked at the increase in the value of their wealth from 2014 to 2018 as an alternative measure of income and measured taxes relative to this increase in wealth. In Buffett's case, over this period, he reported $125 million in regularly measured income on his tax returns and paid $23.7 million in taxes. Using our traditional measure for a tax rate, this would be 19 percent rate of tax ($23.7m/$125m). However, over this same period, Buffett's wealth (primarily the value of his stock in his company) increased by $24.3 billion. Measuring taxes relative to this increase in wealth yields a tax rate of only 0.1 percent ($23.7m/$24.3b)! By this measure, Buffett paid a lower tax rate than Jeff Bezos, Michael Bloomberg and Elon Musk. Musk paid the highest rate in this group, but only 3.3 percent, again using as a basis the increase in his wealth.

Are these the correct rates? Does Warren Buffett pay only one-tenth of 1 percent of his income in taxes? Well, that depends on what we mean by income. The most familiar definition we would use would be the sum of his wages, interest, dividends, capital gains and any other earnings he received. Normally, we would not count the increase in the value of his stock holdings as part of his income. We would only count the increase in the value of his stock holding if he sold the stock—or in tax law jargon—*realized* the income through the sale of his stock. This principle that to be included in income there needs to be some realization event (a sale, for example) has been enshrined in U.S. tax law since a 1920 U.S. Supreme Court case, *Eisner v. Macomber*. Although most legal scholars no longer believe that the U.S. Constitution necessarily requires a realization event to tax income, it has been the general practice for income taxation. So, from a traditional legal point of view, Buffett's tax rate would be 19 percent.

From an economic point of view, the situation appears quite different. When Buffett's stock holdings appreciated, he had additional resources at his command to either consume or to save. According to what is known in economics as the Haig–Simons definition of income, true economic income is the sum of wages plus increases in the value of assets. Increases in the value of assets include appreciation of the assets plus any other payments received from the assets, such as dividends or interest. Under this measure, appreciation of assets even if they are not realized count as income since it provides the individual with additional command over resources. Since Buffett pays himself only a modest salary, his Haig–Simons income would consist primarily of the appreciation in his stock portfolio. The calculation by ProPublica of Buffett's tax rate as 0.1 percent would be an accurate measure of his Haig–Simons effective tax rate.

These alternative calculations raise several important questions. First, which measure of taxes should we use? Should we stay with our traditional legal definition or take the more expansive Haig–Simon version and include appreciation of assets in our measure of income? (Would your answer be the same if for one year, the value of Buffett's holding fell by several billion dollars, and he requested an enormous tax refund?) Second, could we design a tax system that was based on unrealized paper gains or losses? For traded stocks, this seems straightforward, but what about shares in a billion-dollar nontraded private equity firm?

It is possible to devise a scheme to reach Haig–Simons income, at least in theory. U.S. Senator Ron Wyden has developed a system which would use changes in observed prices for traded assets (the so-called mark-to-market taxation system), but for nontraded assets, his system would wait until they are sold and then tax them retrospectively with appropriate interest charges. How this would work in practice and what unanticipated consequences might emerge would be critical issues if this or similar proposals began to be considered seriously. We discuss these and related issues in Chapter 7.

Tax fairness

As a second example exploring the foundations of tax controversies, consider the topic of tax fairness. Sometimes raw political discourse exposes fault lines that carry over into tax debates. Two iconic moments illustrate deep-seated views about work, effort and attribution of success. The first was in 1980. Soon-to-be President Ronald Reagan was campaigning during the Republican primaries and using his campaign funds paid for a New Hampshire newspaper, the *Nashua Telegraph*, to sponsor a debate. Reagan wanted all the candidates to be on the stage, but the debate moderator from the newspaper only wanted the two front-runners—Reagan and George H.W. Bush—to participate. As controversy arose, the moderator tried to cut off Reagan's microphone, but an angry and testy Reagan boomed out, *"I am paying for this microphone, Mr. Green."* Reagan's righteous anger and his unwavering belief that by financing the debate out of his own funds he deserved deference and respect set the stage and tone for his presidency.[11] During the Reagan presidency, what you earned was yours—any taxes that government levied were taking your earnings. Taxes might be necessary, but they were taken from the money that you had earned, and whatever you purchased with your money belonged to you.

Contrast this with remarks given by President Barack Obama during his re-election campaign in 2012. At a rally, he spoke these words to the crowd: "Somebody helped to create this unbelievable American system that we have that allowed you to thrive. Somebody invested in roads and bridges. If you've got a business, you didn't build that."[12] Obama, of course, was not saying that an individual who built a business did not really build it but was referring to the idea that to develop a business or launch a career, we need public goods: private enterprise exists in a social context. Society provided funding for infrastructure and education which, at some level, are preconditions for commerce and social life. Nonetheless, Obama's statement was portrayed by his opponent during the campaign as belittling the accomplishments of entrepreneurs and other working people.

Obama's speech echoed earlier remarks that now-Senator Elizabeth Warren made in 2011. "There is nobody in this country who got rich on his own. Nobody. You built a factory out there? Good for you. But I want to be clear: you moved your goods to market on the roads the rest of us paid for; you hired workers the rest of us paid to educate; you were safe in your factory because of police forces and fire forces that the rest of us paid for."[13]

The remarkably diverse sentiments toward wealth and ownership, embodied in the remarks of U.S. politicians reflect differences in philosophy and psychology. Libertarian thinkers emphasize the role of individual initiative in creating wealth, knowledge and other socially valuable goods, as exemplified by the efforts of entrepreneurs such as Steve Jobs, Mark Zuckerberg, Michael Bloomberg and Bill Gates. On the other hand, the Internet, which provided the infrastructure for the great fortunes of our time, originated through basic research and the development of novel prototype communication networks funded by DARPA, an agency of the Department of Defense. Initiative clearly matters, but it also takes place in a social context.

Stepping back from this debate, we can ask two broader questions. Given that individuals create income and wealth through society, what claims does society have on the fruits of this labor—specifically taxation? And what schemes of taxation are most consistent with basic principles of human psychology, so that whatever tax systems we develop will be accepted by the public as reasonable and fair?

While these questions may seem remote from day-to-day controversies about taxes, they underlie the major debates about tax burdens that regularly flare up in our democracy. The philosophical controversies of distributive justice—exemplified in the twentieth-century work of John Rawls and Robert Nozick—still resonate today.[14] There is a fundamental divide in perspective between the two thinkers: must extraordinary personal financial gains be seen as part of a social dividend that needs to be shared among all members of society (Rawls), or aside from contributions to provide a basic legal and social infrastructure, do the extraordinary rewards belong to individuals (Nozick)?

One issue that reoccurs throughout the book is whether we should focus our distributional concerns on the entire fiscal system—taxes and spending—or just on the tax system. For the moment, let us focus on fairness within the tax system. Even adopting the "tax only" view for judging fairness, there are several unresolved issues. For example, consider proportionate reductions in income tax rates that would apply to all tax brackets. Critics typically claim that the rich would obtain more of the benefits from such policies. In one sense this is certainly true, because the rich are paying more taxes to begin with, so a general rate cut would provide them with higher dollar refunds. Supporters of rate cuts would claim it was fair by focusing on percentage changes in taxes, rather than absolute amounts. But both opponents and proponents are starting from the status quo as a baseline to measure the fairness of tax changes.

Liam Murphy and Thomas Nagel, in their book *The Myth of Ownership,* reject this view.[15] They believe that the status quo is enshrined in the public mind but should have no moral significance. Rather, they advocate for a perspective rooted in Rawlsian ideas of distributive justice where the overall tax system (and perhaps spending system) should be evaluated in its entirety. Whether a tax cut looks favorable to the rich or poor based on absolute dollars or percentage terms does not really matter—it is the final, after-tax distribution of income that we should care about.

Murphy and Nagel attribute our fascination with the status quo to what they term "everyday libertarianism." By this term they mean the presumption that what you earn through work and investing in the market belongs to you and, more importantly, you deserve what you earned. While Murphy and Nagel think this view is untenable (it ignores the social foundations of how you earned your income), it is an idea that has great psychological salience for individuals.

The strong feeling that you deserve what you earn is consistent with "equity theory" a well-established theory in social psychology. Equity theory is a school in psychology based on well-documented evidence that individuals feel more satisfied with themselves and in their relationships with others when the rewards or returns they receive from their actions are related to the inputs or efforts they have made.[16]

Most equity theorists suggest that individuals believe an outcome to be fair when there is some type of equal balance between inputs (effort) and outputs (results). When faced with inequitable situations, individuals can employ two different strategies to make them seem more equitable. First, they can adjust their inputs to restore proportionality, for example, by increasing or decreasing their work efforts. Psychologists found that workers who were led to believe they were "overpaid" would adjust their work effort. Those workers who were compensated on a flat salary basis would put in more hours, while those workers who were paid by piece rate would increase the quality of their efforts.

As an alternative, individuals can restore "psychological equity" by beginning to think of the task or relationship in a different way. For example, in one study participants who were led to believe they were "underpaid" not only reduced their efforts but also began to perceive that they were less qualified than others who were paid more. In related experiments, participants who were "overpaid" reported that they found the task assigned to them more difficult than the tasks assigned to others. Not just effort but also beliefs and expectations can adjust to restore equity in social situations.

Little did Ronald Reagan and Barack Obama realize that their political discourse had such deep philosophical and psychological foundations. Tax debates—the heart of the differences between Republicans and Democrats in the United States—are the surface manifestations of deep divisions in philosophy and psychology.

Taxing corporations

As a third example of deeper foundations for tax controversies, consider the frequent news stories of corporations not paying taxes. These controversies take two forms—domestic and foreign corporations. In neither case are the controversies about illegal behavior on the part of corporations. Rather the controversies reveal much deeper, fundamental issues about the nature of corporate taxation.

On the domestic front, the Institute on Taxation and Economic Policy (ITEP) regularly publishes reports that major U.S. corporations did not pay U.S. income taxes, despite showing positive earnings to their shareholders.

Their most recent report highlighted 55 major U.S. companies that paid no U.S. tax including companies as diverse as FedEx and Nike.[17] These findings were not surprising—the section of their report discussing the results was entitled "Companies' Low Tax Rates Rely on a Variety of Familiar Tax Breaks."

The tax breaks the companies used were all in line with official government policy. They included tax deductions for stock options provided to employees as compensation, deductions for making investments and tax credits for research and development expenses. For both stock options and deductions for investments, the rules for calculating taxes differ from the rules that govern how they are reported for corporate earnings. Congress is aware of these differences. For example, Congress deliberately allowed companies to immediately deduct their investment spending to stimulate investment. Similarly, Congress provided generous credits for research and development expenses to promote innovation. The result of these policies is that companies that invest in capital equipment, engage in extensive R&D and allowed their executives to exercise their stock options, would pay less U.S. tax by design. Sometimes these and other tax incentives would eliminate U.S. corporate taxes; other times they would reduce it, and in many instances, they would simply postpone the taxes to a later date.[18]

While stories about major U.S. corporations that pay no U.S. taxes regularly gain attention in the press, they raise several more basic questions. The first set of questions has to do with the rationale for the corporate tax itself. What is the basic purpose of taxing corporations, apart from the individuals who own or work for the corporations? How does it fit with the regular income tax? Is the primary purpose of the corporate tax to raise revenue, or is the purpose of the corporate tax to indirectly tax the very wealthy?

Alternatively, should the corporate tax be designed to better regulate the behavior of corporations? This was one of the primary motivations for the original corporate tax in the United States in 1909. Depending on the rationale for the corporate tax, is the current structure appropriate or are changes needed to adapt the current corporate tax to better fit with its mission?

Assuming we settled on a rationale for the corporate tax, there is still the issue raised by the ITEP studies: namely, in any given year, many large corporations do not pay U.S. tax. Is this a problem? The public (including the press who regularly publish these stories) does seem to think so. According to the Pew Research Center, 59 percent of the public say they are "bothered a lot" by the fact that corporations do not pay their fair share, while another 22 percent are "bothered some."[19] Respondents expressed similar concerns about wealthy individuals not paying their fair share. However, over longer periods of time, profitable corporations do pay federal income taxes; they also pay income taxes to state and foreign governments and pay sales and payroll taxes.[20] How should we balance the public's concerns with perceived tax unfairness with the reality of global multinationals corporations?

Controversies about corporate taxes are now global, not only local. At a 2012 U.K. parliamentary hearing on the low amount of taxes paid by the largest U.S. multinational corporations in the United Kingdom, Member of Parliament Margaret Hodge delivered one of the great tax quotes of the twenty-first century. In response to a representative of Google who was explaining their global tax structures, she responded: "We are not accusing you of being illegal, we are accusing you of being immoral."[21] Amazon and Starbucks also came under fire. The Members of Parliament were incredulous that Starbucks claimed they were making no profits in the United Kingdom despite their 7,000 employees. U.S. multinationals also faced Congressional ire in the United States. Former Michigan Senator Carl Levin led a series of hearings through the Permanent Subcommittee on Investigations to high-light and explain the international tax structures used by U.S. multinational corporations to avoid taxes. Among the many companies his committee focused on was the iconic U.S. manufacturer of farm equipment, Caterpillar, who used a complicated structure with a newly formed Swiss corporation to sharply reduce its overall worldwide tax bill.[22]

Both the U.K. Parliamentary and the U.S. Senate hearings focused on the emergence of a growth of new strategies whereby multinational corporations could legally avoid taxes by creating a complex web of international corpo-rate structures, all within the same corporate family. While concerns that U.S. corporations were avoiding tax on worldwide income date back at least to the 1960s, this problem exploded in the first decade of the twenty-first cen-tury. The rapid growth and scale of multinational corporations, their aggres-sive tax posture and the creativity of their tax advisors, initially outstripped the ability of nation states to comprehend these strategies and forced them to re-design their own tax structures to better meet the challenge posed to their fiscal systems. In the last several years, countries have taken a variety of actions to preserve their tax base.

These are not the only issues underlying international tax controversies today. Starbucks may be paying more taxes in the United Kingdom today, but the United Kingdom and other European countries do not believe that they are receiving enough revenue from companies like Facebook who have little physical presence but make substantial profits from advertising to Facebook users. The Organization for Economic Co-operation and Development (OECD) has been leading a major project that would re-allocate some tax revenue toward countries where consumers reside. These discussions may eventually lead to a new system for international taxation, but they also raise deeper issues. Is it a question of fairness—do countries where consumers reside deserve to tax the profits of Facebook and other multinationals? Or is this a better way to think of where "value is created," as the OECD at one point proclaimed?[23] Many of the most sophisticated international tax economists reject allocating tax revenue based on fairness or where value is created but do endorse allocating some revenue to countries where consumers are located on efficiency grounds.[24] Consumers, after all, cannot easily change their locations—unlike mobile international firms and intellectual property. Other leading international economists, such as Mihir Desai, believe that the worst abuses of the corporate tax system are behind us, that traditional mechanisms for allocating profits across countries—the so-called transfer pricing methods—can now be a reasonable framework for the future, and that there is no need for a radical restructuring of the system.[25]

Plan for the Book

As we have seen, our three examples of modern controversies—taxing billionaires, the contours of tax fairness and taxing domestic and international corporations—all require deeper structural analysis to understand the true nature of the controversy. Whether it is to determine "who gets what" or to understand the psychological and sociological aspects of tax controversies, it is necessary to go beyond the surface and uncover the roots of the underlying controversies. The subsequent chapters in the book do just that.

Chapter 2 takes a close look at the conventional wisdom of having a broad income tax base and low rates. At least in the United States, tax reform is associated with the Tax Reform Act of 1986, which aimed to eliminate deductions and exclusions and lower rates. However, this reform did not last long. This chapter explains the economic and political contours of broad base-low-rate policies. It discusses the economic concept of excess burden and how designing a system to minimize excess burden may not be consistent with conventional wisdom. From an economic point of view, the case for a broad base and low rates is surprisingly weak. This can account for the disappearance of broad base-low rates, despite their superficial appeal. The chapter also discusses both the politics and economics of tax expenditures.

Chapter 3 explores the important issue of whether income that is saved should be included in the tax base. Many of the complexities of the tax system stem from exclusions for savings from the tax base, for example, for retirement accounts, as well as lower tax rates for capital income. The key question is whether the tax system should aim to reach comprehensive income (which would include capital income derived from savings) or focus more directly on consumption. The U.S. tax system is a hybrid with both features. This chapter explores the efficiency rationale for a consumption tax and alternative ways to tax consumption. Despite some apparent efficiency advantages, the changes that would need to accompany either a thoroughgoing pure income or consumption tax are beyond the capacity of most political systems.

I return to corporate taxation in Chapter 4. The taxation of multinational corporations has taken on a theological importance in today's tax debates. Despite a relative constant share of tax revenue from corporations over the past several decades, the unseemly tax minimization practices of some multinationals in the recent past have triggered populist reaction in many countries. Reforms to the international tax system several years ago have removed some of its worst features, but the demand for a radical restructuring continues. Is the current system broken or can marginal changes make it work effectively? Is the underlying basis for the current system of international taxation workable in today's economy? Are there any lessons we can learn from U.S. state taxation of multinational corporations?

Chapter 5 takes a deeper dive into tax fairness. There are two broad perspectives on tax fairness. The first is the overall distributional view of taxes—who gets what. Most day-to-day discussions of tax policy fall within this model. The philosophical foundations of this view which situates it in larger theories of social justice is exemplified in the work of Murphy and Nagel. An alternative view focuses on the psychological relations that individuals have to the tax and economic system, what has been termed "folk justice." The psychological theories of procedural justice (being treated according to well-defined rules and with respect) and equity theory (net returns should be based on effort) can explain popular perceptions of taxes and situations when taxes seem unfair. The tension between these views is at the heart of tax policy disputes. The chapter also discusses whether it is feasible to base a tax system on concepts other than general welfare—such as whether we can tax individuals on their desert or deservingness, and also recent work by economists to incorporate nontraditional ideas into their models of taxation.

Chapter 6 tackles a topic that has recently received increased attention in the United States—whether the tax system has a built-in racial bias. It is difficult to address this question as tax information—unlike Census data—does not contain explicit racial information. Nonetheless, some have argued that structural features of the tax system—such as the marriage penalty or bonus or tax benefits from owning property—accrue to certain racial groups based on their socioeconomic profiles. This chapter sorts through this debate and raises the question of whether racial equity problems are inherent in the structure of taxes or are a result of choices of the benefits that our political system delivers through the tax system.

Earlier in this chapter, I raised some conceptual issues about taxing the wealthy. In Chapter 7, we probe this topic in more detail. The apparent increase in inequality of income and wealth in recent years has motivated novel approaches to attempt to tax the very rich, although the data are not as conclusive as popular (and some academic) accounts suggest. The chapter first explains the contested data and the controversies surrounding them. It then surveys the history of taxing the rich, noting that major changes have only occurred around wars but can persist for some time after. I then explore alternative ways to tax appreciation in assets, including both through income taxation and wealth taxation. Wealth taxation has had only limited success in Europe and faces potential constitutional obstacles in the United States. There are more options for taxing appreciation of property, but they all will require fundamental changes in basic principles of income taxation, especially the realization principle. These changes are potentially feasible but will be technically challenging and politically difficult. Lastly, I will discuss more modest reforms to our estate and gift tax regime.

In our final chapter, I return to the basic theme of this book and review the underlying social, legal and economic factors that are below the surface of our tax controversies. These nicely fall into social, legal/administrative and economic categories. I then step back from our detailed investigations and raise some broader issues about the tax system. First are questions of how we use the tax system for social ends and whether in doing so we risk not being able to ensure fiscal adequacy. Second, I explore a set of issues around taxation and democracy. What control should the public have over tax policy in the face of increasing globalization and increasing international agreements? Should an international expert class determine the directions of national or international tax policy, or should the views and votes of the residents of the nation be the chief determinant of fiscal matters?

Notes

1 These issues are addressed fully in Sheffrin, *Tax Fairness and Folk Justice*. The focus of this book is on the deeper structure of tax policy debates, although one chapter does discuss philosophical and psychological foundations.
2 See, for example, Raphael, "Debunking Tea Party Myths."
3 Tax Policy Center, "How Many People Pay the Estate Tax?"
4 Bowman, "Public Opinion on Taxes." Examples include the Roper poll in 1935 and the Kaiser-Kennedy School poll in 2003.
5 Graetz and Shapiro, *Death by a Thousand Cuts* and Sheffrin, *Tax Fairness and Folk Justice*, probe this issue.
6 Quote from Richards, "An Expressive Theory of Tax," quote at 313.
7 See Sheffrin, *Tax Fairness and Folk Justice*, Chapter 1.

8 See Backman, "Why Does Billionaire Warren Buffet Pay a Lower Tax Rate Than His Secretary?"

9 This implies that the average tax rate for millionaires is not sufficiently different from 30 percent to make a large revenue difference. For one account, see Williams, "Taxing Millionaires, Obama's Buffet Rule."

10 Eisenger et al. "The Secret IRS Files: Trove of Never-Before-Seen Records Reveal How the Wealthiest Avoid Income Tax."

11 For an account of the entire episode, see Dufresne, "Ronald Reagan's Testy Moment in the 1980 GOP Debate."

12 For a defense of this quote and a discussion of the campaign, see Weiner, "The Rise of Romney's 'You Didn't Build This' Meme."

13 A video of her speech and a description are at Warren, "You Didn't Build That" Speech.

14 See, Rawls, *The Theory of Justice* and Nozick, *Anarchy, State, and Utopia*.

15 Murphy and Nagel, *The Myth of Ownership*.

16 See Sheffrin, *Tax Fairness and Folk Justice*, Chapter 2.

17 ITEP, "55 Corporations Paid $0 in Federal Taxes on 2020 Profits."

18 To attempt to address this issue, the Congress enacted a minimum tax on corporations based on their book accounting measures. However, there were many exceptions, such as allowing rapid depreciation and tax credits for green energy, so it is not clear what effect this will ultimately have on the perception problem of reports of zero taxes paid in a given year.

19 The Pew study found, however, that there were also wide partisan gaps in concerns over whether corporations pay their fair share in taxes. See Pew Research Center, "Top Tax Frustrations for Americans."

20 For a thorough discussion of the evidence of taxes paid using financial accounting data, see Dyreng and Hanlon, "Tax Avoidance and Multinational Firm Behavior."

21 Syal, "Amazon, Google, and Starbucks Accused of Diverting UK Profits."

22 See United States Senate, Permanent Subcommittee on Investigations, "Caterpillar's Offshore Tax Strategy."

23 The OECD at one point linked transfer pricing reforms to better reflect where value is created. See OECD, "Aligning Transfer Pricing Outcomes with Value Creation."

24 See Deveraux et al., *Taxing Profit in a Global Economy* for two proposals that rely at least in part on where customers are located.

25 Desai, "Myths and Mysteries of the Corporate Income Tax."

Chapter 2

THE RISE AND FALL OF
CLASSIC TAX REFORM

If you polled the informed public—legislators, lawyers, economists and the press—on the most impressive tax bill enacted in the United States within recent memory, the majority verdict would almost certainly be the Tax Reform Act of 1986 (TRA). Since the law was enacted more than 36 years ago the details might be vague for most people, but the positive feelings from the bill persist. Some readers may have encountered the entertaining triumphant political saga and definitive political account of the passage of the bill, *Showdown in Gucci Gulch*.[1] Others may recall the TRA portrayed as a reform that eliminated loopholes and special preferences and brought down tax rates on all income to 28 percent.[2]

Importantly, the TRA would embed itself in the public's mind as a concrete instance where the primary mantra of all tax reforms—broad base and low rates—was actually put into practice. According to this tenet, sound tax policy should tax all income equally and at the same rate, and not award special deductions or tax incentives for any types of economic activity. It is an easy maxim to preach but putting it into practice is much more difficult. This chapter provides a critical examination of the doctrine of broad base and low rates.

What Did the Tax Reform Act Do?

In practice, the TRA did many different things. One of the most important was to eliminate most of the tax shelters that had sprung up in the early 1980s which had threatened the viability of the tax system. These tax shelters consisted of businesses with dubious economic bona fides and included, among other investments, chinchilla farms, jojoba bean plantings and computers to design personalized diets. They were built primarily on tax deductions stemming from borrowed money and rapid depreciation write-offs of equipment and buildings, promising tax savings in just a few years that would exceed any initial investment. They were no longer the province of the rich but had begun to reach into the upper-middle and middle-class.[3] Not only were these a threat to the actual tax collections of the federal government, but they also drew an unsavory collection of tax entrepreneurs into a growing tax avoidance industry and bred a corrosive cynicism among ordinary taxpayers toward the tax system in general. The TRA eliminated the bulk of these shelters through new and complex rules on "passive losses," preventing taxpayers from claiming tax losses on the shelters to offset their regular income.[4]

The TRA also reduced or eliminated other types of deductions. For example, the deduction on interest on personal loans was phased out, limits on deductions for business meals and entertainment were imposed, unemployment insurance became taxable and the deduction for state and local sales taxes was eliminated.[5] Parents now had to supply the Social Security numbers for their children, thereby preventing exemptions for phantom dependents; as a result, about 7 million children disappeared from tax returns.[6] While these provisions had both supporters and detractors, the justification for their inclusion in the bill was understandable. Moreover, the value of the deductions that remained in the law was reduced because of the reduction in marginal tax rates. A charitable deduction of $1,000 generates tax savings of $500 at a 50 percent tax rate, but only a $280 tax savings at a 28 percent rate.

More controversial, however, were some other key provisions of the TRA. Contributions to individual retirement accounts (IRAs) were sharply limited and re-targeted to lower-income households and those without pension plans. While these changes raised revenue, they also decreased incentives for individuals to save. At the business level, the investment tax credit—a direct subsidy for new investment spending—was eliminated. No longer would a $1,000 investment in new equipment cost just $900 after a 10 percent credit. Firms were also required to depreciate or write off the value of their assets more slowly. This reduced the present value of their tax savings, as the tax savings occurred further in the future. Again, these actions raised substantial revenue for the federal government. While the TRA was supposedly revenue neutral as a package, it raised revenue from the corporate sector, despite reductions in corporate tax rates, to provide net tax savings to households. These business tax changes immediately affected certain industries, such as commercial real estate, which had always relied on generous tax treatment, but they also had a more general effect of reducing the incentives for new investment.

Perhaps the most controversial change of all was the elimination of a lower tax rate for long-term capital gains (increases in the value of assets). With the passage of the TRA, all capital gains from stock holdings or other sources were taxed at the same rate as wage or other ordinary income, regardless of how long they were held. The top rate on long-term gains was 28 percent, just as for other types of income. Proponents of this change highlighted the fact that wealthy taxpayers were the ones that earned income from capital gains; now they would be paying at the same rate as wage earners. As a result, owners of capital and wage earners would be treated equally. Moreover, there would be less of an incentive to try to find clever ways to convert ordinary wage income into capital income so that it could be taxed at a lower rate.

Opponents of this change, however, warned that lower tax rates for long-term capital gains were in the tax code for a reason. When assets were sold and generated capital gains, some of that gain was simply due to general inflation and did not represent a real gain to the seller. The government was in fact just taxing illusory, inflationary gains. Investments are also risky and to encourage long-term investing, they maintained there must be a sufficient incentive—the lower tax rate on long-term capital gains provided such an incentive.

Maintaining the capital gains rate equal to the rate on ordinary income also had implications for how progressive the tax system could be. There are limits to how high taxes can be on capital gains. If the rate is too high, individuals will simply not sell their assets. In the United States at that time and continuing through today, capital gains on assets are effectively eliminated at death through a provision known as "step-up in basis." No capital gains taxes are due from heirs who inherit the assets, no matter how much the assets rose in value. This provision in the law has the consequence that if capital gains rates are raised too high, individuals will simply not sell and hold on to their assets until they die. Moreover, if they can borrow against the value of their assets, as billionaires routinely do today to finance their consumption, they effectively execute the "buy, borrow and die" strategy to avoid taxation on appreciated assets.[7] Raising rates too high will actually reduce government revenue. At least for capital gains, there is a revenue-maximizing capital gains rate. If the rate is higher than that, the government loses revenues.[8]

The fact that tax rates on capital gains cannot be too high without unintended consequences limits the ability to simultaneously maintain equality between the taxes on wages and capital gains and to also have sharply progressive taxes on wage income. The top tax rate in the TRA at 28 percent was substantially lower than the 50 percent rate that prevailed before the law was passed. Since 1993, the top tax rate on ordinary income has ranged from 35 to 39.6 percent, lower than the 50 percent rate prior to the TRA, but clearly higher than the 28 percent rate in the TRA. Some recent estimates for the capital gains that would maximize revenue do reach as high as the 35 to 39.6 percent range, but the consensus estimates are lower. For example, the Urban-Brookings Tax Policy Center uses models with a revenue-maximizing rate of 28 percent rate, which is consistent with the estimates from the Joint

Committee on Taxation.[9] In any case, steeply progressive personal income taxes might not be feasible if the long-term capital gains rate had to march in lock-step with the tax rate on ordinary income.

In 2021, President Joe Biden's administration did propose to tax capital gains at the same rate as ordinary income at 39.6 percent (plus some other surtaxes). The administration believed that they only could do this if they ended step-up in basis so that capital gains would automatically be taxed upon death. That would reduce the incentive to hold onto appreciated stocks even when tax rates increased. They tried to make this dramatic change in the U.S. tax law palatable by having it only apply to taxpayers whose joint income exceeded $1 million. They also suggested that there should be provisions to defer the taxes for small businesses and farms if they were kept in the family. However, their proposal met with opposition from many quarters, and to the dismay of many liberals and progressives, even the House Ways and Means Committee, controlled by the Democratic party, did not include eliminating step-up in basis in their initial legislation. But without the step-up in basis, the equality of tax rates on capital gains and ordinary income was perhaps a bridge too far—the Ways and Means Committee proposed a lower rate on capital gains than on ordinary income.

Despite these controversies, the TRA received an incredibly positive reception at the time. It was viewed as a "political miracle," given the history of special interest legislation. One of the authors of *Showdown at Gucci Gulch* remarked that it succeeded, although the key players were not initially enthusiastic about tax reform, but they were simply too afraid to let it die and incur the public wrath.[10] President Reagan remarked that it was "the best anti-poverty measure, the best pro-family measure and the best job-creation measure ever to come out of the Congress of the United States."[11] There were some skeptics shortly thereafter. Michael Graetz, a distinguished tax academic and policy maker decried the hyperbole associated with the TRA, even by academics who typically were more critical of legislation. However, even he did not deny its political significance, placing its political impact as at "least a 9.1 if we had a Richter scale for that sort of thing."[12]

But despite all the political drama and accolades from politicians and academics, a key feature of the TRA did not last very long at all. Despite campaign promises to "read my lips, no new taxes," President George H.W. Bush in 1991 raised the top rate on ordinary income to 31 percent, keeping the capital gains rate at 28 percent. By 1993, President Bill Clinton raised the rate on ordinary income to 39.6 percent maintaining the capital gains rate again at 28 percent. The TRA experiment maintaining the equality of tax rates for capital and ordinary income thus ended abruptly. Over the years, other major changes occurred as well. With President George W. Bush, depreciation deductions for new investments were accelerated and dividends, which were previously taxed as ordinary income, were now taxed at the lower capital gains rate.

Why did the 1986 experiment meet its demise?

Why Did Broad Base Low Rates Not Survive After the Tax Reform Act?

A political explanation

One of the first explanations for the demise of the 1986 Tax Reform Act came from the economist Milton Friedman. As early as 1978, Milton Friedman put forward his own theory about why the tax system was so complicated.[13] In his view, it was politicians who would raise campaign funds either by promising tax relief to constituencies or, alternatively, offering to protect them from tax increases proposed by other lawmakers. The campaign finance system was simply too lucrative to change—as a result over time the tax system became more complex. Stanley Winer and Walter Hettich offered a related but more formally academic argument for the proliferation of special features and preferences in the tax system.[14] Politicians could "price discriminate" by tailoring preferences to specific constituencies. Both theories suggested that tax reform—which would mean precisely eliminating these special preferences—was not compatible with the current political system.

How then did Milton Friedman explain the Tax Reform Act? According to Friedman, during tax reform, the Senate Finance Committee led by Senator Robert Packwood initially tried to award more tax preferences, but during their deliberations "discovered that this process had come to a dead end. As it were, the tax space was overcrowded with loopholes."[15] Writing at the time, Friedman argues that Senator Packwood's radical gambit to eliminate scores of tax preferences "wipes the slate clean, thereby providing space for the tax reform cycle to start over again."[16] In other words, by eliminating many preferences in the tax code, the Congress set the stage for future demands for new breaks and/or new protections for their constituencies. In Friedman's view, the rather sudden demise of the key principles of the Tax Reform Act was not a surprise, but an inevitable outcome of the structure of the U.S. political system. Friedman did not assert that Senator Packwood or the other members of Congress were fully aware of what they were doing, but according to his theory, it was fully in their interests.

Sometimes a theory is too neat to be true. Friedman's theory was that once the slate was wiped clean through tax reform, Congress would go back to their usual business of generating campaign cash and that explains why the reform did not stick. What Friedman's theory leaves out was the other primary concern of Congress during that period—deficit reduction. Fears of deficits plagued the Congress during this period. In 1985, the Congress enacted the first of a series of deficit control measures, the Gramm–Rudman–Hollings Act that set goals for deficit reduction and built enforcement measures into Congressional procedure.[17] The Tax Reform Act was designed to be revenue neutral and did not deal with the deficit. It was deficit concerns that led President George H.W. Bush to renege on his tax pledge, opening the initial divergence between tax rates for capital gains and ordinary income. Once that happened, further rounds of tax increases were inevitable. Congress, of course, could resume business as usual with campaign contributions resuming once the sanctity of the Tax Reform Act was breached, but deficit fears rather than political machinations provide an alternative purely political explanation for the rapid demise of the Tax Reform Act.

TRA was economically inefficient

An alternative explanation for evolution of tax policy away from the Tax Reform Act was that that it had its economics wrong. Broad base and low rates, while a simple slogan, is not a recipe for economic efficiency—instead, this policy causes important economic distortions to which the tax system must eventually adjust.

The Economics of excess burden

To understand this perspective, we need to explore a few principles from the economics of taxation. If the government decides it wants to raise $1m from the private sector through taxation, there clearly will be a burden of at least $1m to the private sector, funds that the private sector will no longer have at their disposal. But depending on how the government decides to raise that $1m, there could be an additional burden.

Consider an example. Suppose that the government wants to raise the $1m by putting a tax on suppliers of cars. In the face of that tax, the sellers of cars will raise their prices, and with the higher prices, consumers will purchase fewer cars. Compared to the situation with no tax, fewer cars are sold in the market. If the number of cars that were sold prior to the imposition of the tax were the appropriate amount—given the costs of producing cars and the demand for cars—then the tax causes too few cars to be transacted in the market. This is a loss both to the producers and consumers of cars. This loss is an additional burden over and above the $1m the government raises in taxes. Economists call this additional cost the excess burden of a tax.

Continuing with our example, suppose that car prices without taxes were initially $30,000. At that price, the last consumer to purchase a car at this price (the marginal consumer) would be willing to pay just $30,000. The last (or marginal) supplier of cars who would just be willing to participate in the market could incur no higher cost than $30,000. At the market price, the last consumer values the car at the marginal cost of production, which is economically efficient. Now let the government place a tax on the producers of cars of $2,000 and assume that car producers can raise prices by $1,000. Car prices in the market are now $31,000 and the producers, after paying the tax, receive $29,000. It is no longer the case that the last consumer, who now pays $31,000, pays precisely what it costs the car manufacturers to produce an additional car. Consumers who value cars more than $30,000 but less than $31,000 are no longer in the market, and car producers earn less profit from not meeting this demand. This loss to both consumers and producers reflects the excess burden of the tax.

One other way to understand excess burden is that taxes typically cause people to change their behavior. To the extent that new taxes cause them to move away from their preferred position prior to the tax, this causes a reduction in their well-being—this is the excess burden of the tax. The more individuals or firms respond to taxes, the greater will be the excess burden. So, if some activities are very sensitive (economists use the term "elastic") to tax changes, the excess burden from levying taxes will be very large. On the other hand, if individuals or firms are not very sensitive (inelastic) and do not change their behavior very much in response to tax changes, the excess burden of the tax will be small.

One last result from the economics of taxation is that excess burden rises rapidly with an increase in taxes. Specifically, it rises with square of the tax rate. Doubling the tax rate from 10 percent to 20 percent will raise the excess burden by a factor of four. Therefore, there are sharp penalties from rapidly increasing tax rates.

Summarizing the economics: Excess burden is the loss to the economy over and above any revenue collected. Taxes cause an excess burden if they change behavior compared to the no tax world. This is a loss in economic efficiency. The more sensitive or elastic behavior is to taxes, the greater the excess burden; conversely, if behavior is not sensitive to taxes, excess burden will be lower. Finally, the amount of excess burden rises steeply and with the square of the tax rate.

Excess burden meets broad base and low rates

We can apply these core economic ideas to evaluate whether the broad base low-rate policy is sound economics in terms of minimizing the total excess burden from taxation. As a starting point, broadening the base and lowering rates does avoid the steep rise in excess burden from increasing tax rates. That is a positive factor in its favor. Low rates generally are a good thing.

However, a broad base low-rate policy treats all economic activities the same, regardless of how sensitive (or elastic) they are to tax changes. This runs counter to economic principles. If we want to reduce the total excess burden from taxation, it would be better to tax activities that are very sensitive to taxation at lower rates and those activities that are not sensitive to taxation at higher rates. In other words, economic efficiency suggests that tax rates should not be uniform. This is an argument against broad base low rates— some activities could be taxed at higher rates to tax other activities at lower rates—or even to subsidize them. The economist Frank Ramsey developed this theory in the 1920s for the taxation of commodities, suggesting that certain commodities should be taxed at higher rates than others to minimize the excess burden of taxation, but the same general principles can be applied to the design of the income tax.[18]

Let us take a simple example to illustrate the potential use of this theory for the income tax. We will start by focusing on deductions from the income tax. Should contributions to charity be allowed as deductions from the income tax? Let us assume that you believe that charitable contributions are beneficial to society. Still, allowing a deduction for charitable contributions means that the government must raise tax rates on other economic activity to raise the same amount of money. What might offset the disadvantage of higher rates?

One question you might want to ask is whether the deduction for charitable contributions is very sensitive to taxes—would people contribute the same amount without the tax break or does the tax break generate substantial new charitable contributions? If people gave the same amount to charity regardless of the tax consequences, there would be no point in allowing a charitable deduction; it would just be a windfall to the givers and raise everyone else's tax rates. On the other hand, if charitable deductions increased sharply with tax breaks, one might consider the loss in revenue and higher tax rates for others potentially worth it to generate the increase in charitable contributions.

Evidence on this issue could potentially be useful in making a policy judgment. Many economic studies have explored the matter and some of the most reputable suggest that charitable giving is sensitive to tax preferences. In many studies, a $1 loss in tax revenue would induce more than $1 in additional giving.[19] This type of evidence, while suggestive, should not necessarily be definitive, as one might want to ask what income groups benefit the most from tax policies that favor charitable giving. Are all charitable contributions the same? Are these preferences just going to the rich who donate artworks to museums or create their own private foundations? What about the loyal church goers who give each week but do not itemize on their tax returns and receive neither an incentive to donate nor any additional benefit? These considerations sometimes get overlooked when economic studies trumpet the increase in charitable giving from tax preferences. But it does make us think that the sensitivity of economic activity to taxes might be a factor we would want to consider in evaluating policy.

The same general principles can be applied to other tax incentives. Should we subsidize historical preservation in cities? How about preserving rural land through conservation easements? On the business side, should research and development expenditures be encouraged through special tax breaks? In all these cases, one can argue both sides of the issue, namely that the activity generates some social good, but that certain activity would occur without the tax incentive.

Take the case of subsidies for research and development and the diffusion of knowledge. Large companies will invest in research and development if they believe it is the path to generate new products and profits. But would more research and development help the economy through spillovers in knowledge? If so, how sensitive is research and development expenditures to tax incentives? Is the additional activity that might be generated worth the cost in higher tax rates for others? If, on balance, the tax incentives are very potent, then we may want to deviate from our broad base low-rate philosophy and provide tax incentives.

One of the more controversial deductions in the U.S. income tax over the years has been the deduction for state and local taxes. The Tax Reform Act of 1986 eliminated deductions for sales taxes, but not for income or property taxes paid to states or localities. Although some reformers wanted to eliminate them as they would allow substantial overall tax rate reductions, the political opposition was too great. Normally, this deduction is discussed as a fairness issue—if individuals pay state and local taxes, they have less ability to pay federal taxes as they have lower disposable income. In 2017, a Republican-controlled Congress with a Republican president succeeded in placing a cap on the state and local tax deduction at $10,000 through 2025, This was particularly impactful in the high-tax states of the Northeast (New York, New Jersey, Connecticut) and the West (California and Oregon). The ensuing debate was largely about the fairness of this policy and its disparate impacts across the states.

Even this issue, which appears on its surface to be about fairness, can be recast as an economic efficiency issue. As James Hines has argued, some types of spending in the states on areas such as education or infrastructure have positive spillover effects to other states and to the national economy.[20] Better roads in California promote interstate commerce and can raise income throughout the country. Thus, there is a positive benefit to such spending. If so, one question becomes whether allowing a state and local tax deduction will lead to higher state spending on education and infrastructure.

Turning away from deductions to tax rates, the first and foremost example of a type of income that is very sensitive to tax rates is capital gains. Individuals have the option to sell or hold their assets and if they simply hold them, the government generates no revenue. Under the current rules that allow capital gains to vanish at death, if rates become too high individuals will be reluctant to sell assets and will instead hold them to pass onto their heirs. In this case in addition to not generating any revenue, high rates may also lock the individual into asset holdings which may not be desirable from their point of view. For example, they may hold on to assets that are too risky, not risky enough or do not fit well into their overall portfolio. Of course, Congress could eliminate the step-up in basis rules, which would diminish the incentive to hold onto assets, but to date that change has proven too controversial.

In recent times, except for the period directly following the Tax Reform Act, the capital gains tax rate has been below the rate on ordinary income. While tax reformers may bemoan the seemingly adverse distributional and efficiency outcomes that result, the stubborn fact that capital gains revenue is highly sensitive to tax rates limits the feasible reform options.

In Chapter 3, we will look more closely at the range of issues involved in taxing income from capital, which also encompasses incentives for savings and investment. As a starting point, the sensitivity of this type of income to tax rates will be an essential component of our analysis.

Even the broad base is too narrow

While not directly responsible for the demise of the TRA, there is another fundamental problem with the broad base low-rate doctrine. For a variety of reasons, our income tax base may not be sufficiently broad, and what we call a "broad base" depends on a variety of practical factors.

In the opening chapter we saw that even how we define income for tax purposes is subject to important debate. Increases in the value of assets—such as appreciated stocks—are not counted as income under our current tax laws unless the assets are sold, that is, until the income is, in tax jargon, realized. Simply holding onto a stock that has gone up in value does not generate income for tax purposes. But from an economic vantage point, the owner of the appreciated stock has increased his or her wealth and consequently has an additional command over resources. As we discussed in Chapter 1, under the Haig–Simons definition of income—wages plus the change in the value of assets—unrealized gains should be counted as income.[21]

This raises the fundamental question: should a broad base include unrealized capital gains? Under our current practice, it does not, but nothing in the word "broad" would necessarily exclude them. There are principled reasons for not taxing unrealized gains and it may be sound tax policy, but the exclusion of unrealized gains by themselves casts a cloud over our conventional definition of a broad base.

Moving away from taxing income from capital and the very wealthy, let us consider workers. Our conventional notion of a broad base focuses on market transactions so that all wage income should be subject to tax. That would include other types of compensation, including fringe benefits such as employer-provided health care or parking, both of which are not currently included in taxable income. But our concept of a broad base does not include the value of leisure time, which clearly has value for employees. The ostensible reason for excluding the value of leisure activities is that it does not directly produce any market income that could be easily taxed, and it would be nearly impossible to value otherwise.[22] No income tax has ever tried to reach the value of leisure time.

However, excluding leisure from a comprehensive broad-base income tax does have important consequences. Consider a young male who is currently not employed but thinking of joining the workforce if he receives a sufficiently high wage. Suppose an employer offers him a wage just slightly above his reservation level and he decides to take a job. To take the job means forgoing leisure activity which he values highly. While his earnings in the new job offset the loss in leisure—which is why he took the job—the increase in his well-being should be measured not by the wage income he receives, but the wage income net of the loss of his leisure time. From that point of view, he may only be slightly better off. Yet, he pays tax on the full amount of his wage income—not his net gain.

There are two economic consequences from our current system of taxation of taxing work: first, it creates a disincentive to work because work is taxed, but leisure is not. If the tax rate is 50 percent, then to sacrifice a dollar worth of leisure will require two dollars in wages. The choice to work versus take leisure time is distorted relative to the no-tax world. Second, it does seem unfair. Why should the young man pay taxes on the full amount of his wages when his welfare—measured net of the value of his leisure—only went up slightly?

As a practical matter, though, trying to tax the young man on the net change of his welfare would eviscerate our income tax system. We would collect virtually no taxes from individuals who are, as many people are, on the margin between working or not. In fact, the net gain for someone literally on the margin of working or not is zero because their earnings from working just counterbalance their loss of leisure. For those individuals who always prefer working, the government would collect less revenue if it somehow subtracted out their loss in leisure time. Nothing in the concept of a broad base tax automatically implies that we place no value on leisure activities. They clearly matter to individuals but recognizing them in normal income tax settings would not allow us to run a well-functioning revenue system.

There are other less obvious examples of our failure to include what could be considered income in our working definition of a broad base. One classic example is what is called imputed rental income for homeowners. If someone owns their house, they are effectively saving on paying the rent that they would otherwise have to pay on the market. One way to think of homeownership is as "renting" the house to oneself. Although no cash changes hands, as the owner of the house, these implicit rental payments could be considered income. Indeed, in one of its formal reports, the U.S, Treasury counts this as income that it imputes to household and on which they do not pay tax.[23]

Another example in the Haig–Simon's spirit would be the income consequences of changing health status. If someone in their mid-40s is diagnosed with cancer and their life expectancy subsequently drops, the value of their future income also drops. This is a decrease in their expected wealth and, according to the Haig–Simon's definition, should be recorded as a drop in their current income. If the diagnosis is suddenly reversed, their Haig–Simon's income would increase, returning to its prior value. Should our broad-based definition of income include these unconventional Haig–Simon revaluations of future income?

These debates are not purely academic. Ever since the 1960s, tax reformers have been interested in trying to quantify deviations from a broad base tax. Various agencies in the United States, government and abroad have developed what are known as tax expenditure budgets to highlight and measure departures from a broad-based income tax. What light can these tax expenditure budgets shed on the desirability and feasibility of broad base-low-rate taxation?

What Can We Learn from Tax Expenditure Budgets?

With a desire to promote reform in the tax code, President John F. Kennedy appointed Harvard professor Stanley Surrey as the Assistant Secretary for Tax Policy, the top tax position at the U.S. Treasury. Surrey brought passion and his keen intellect to the task of reforming the tax code. One of his chief innovations was to develop and popularize the concept of tax expenditures.

According to Surrey, tax expenditures were government spending that rather than flowing through the normal congressional appropriations process instead were delivered through the tax system. For example, instead of giving a direct cash subsidy to homeowners, the government provides a deduction for the mortgage interest that is paid. Tax expenditures can be implemented in several different ways: through income that is simply excluded from taxes, deductions that are granted before calculating taxable income, or with tax credits that provide direct dollar for dollar offsets of tax liability. Rather than just being another vehicle to deliver government spending to the public, Surrey argued that this system was perverse and had unintended consequences.

Consider the mortgage interest deduction, which allowed taxpayers who itemize their deductions—instead of taking a flat standard deduction—to deduct interest payments before calculating taxable income. The intention of this tax provision was to subsidize homeownership, even though other countries, such as Canada, saw no need for such a policy. Surrey highlighted several problems with this policy. First, the benefits tended to accrue primarily to higher income households who were more likely to own a house rather than rent. Second, even within the home-owning class, the subsidy was greater for higher-income households than lower-income households. A high-income household in the 50 percent tax bracket would save $50 for every $100 of mortgage interest, while a middle-income household in the 30 percent bracket would only save $30 for the same interest costs. This is an "upside down subsidy" and, as Surrey noted, not something that any legislature would ever dare endorse as part of a direct spending program. Finally, once this provision was put into the tax code, it would stay in place until it was repealed. It was thus an open-ended subsidy with no clear termination date; there would be no natural point to review or assess the program.

What could be done to improve this situation? One improvement would be for deductions, which provide upside-down subsidies, to be converted to tax credits. With a tax credit for mortgage interest, all taxpayers could be given for example a 20 percent credit, that is, a $20 reduction in taxes for $100 of mortgage interest expense. This would treat all homeowners equally. These credits could also be scheduled to sunset at some point so that future tax writing committees would have to re-authorize the credit. For some programs, such as credits for historical rehabilitation, there also could be an application process to qualify and a limit placed on the total tax credits awarded. With these or similar reforms, tax expenditures would be subject to similar reviews as normal expenditure programs.

Surrey's advocacy for reform led eventually to Congress mandating in 1974 that a tax expenditure budget be created and published to list all spending-like programs through the tax system and to estimate their cost in terms of lost revenue to the government. The U.S. Treasury, representing the executive branch and the Joint Committee on Taxation, representing Congress, each publish their own estimates.

Tax expenditures were defined as departures from a "normal" income tax system. That meant that items not included in taxable income—such as unrealized capital gains—were not listed as tax expenditures. On the other hand, since the baseline for measuring tax reform was a "normal" income tax that would tax interest, dividends, capital gains and other capital income, any tax preferences or reduced tax rates for these items of income would be counted as tax expenditures.

For advocates of a broad base low-rate policy, the tax expenditure budget would be prime hunting grounds for tax reform. But a careful look at the top tax expenditures will dampen the enthusiasm of even the strongest broad base advocates. Let us take a close look at the top 10 tax expenditures in 2021 according to the Urban-Brookings Tax Policy Center.[24]

The number one tax expenditure on all the lists throughout the years is the exclusion for employee sponsored health insurance. When employers pay health insurance premiums for their employees, those payments are not included in employees' taxable income. This is by far the largest tax expenditure, but it is such an essential part of the U.S. health care system that eliminating it would be politically unfeasible. A full discussion of health care alternatives is beyond our scope here—but given the difficulties the United System has had with even modest health care reform, this tax preference is here to stay. Item number nine, the subsidies to purchase insurance through the Affordable Care Act marketplace, are also not likely to be removed.

Several of the top tax expenditures deal with preferences given to capital income and the returns from savings. These include reduced tax rates for capital gains (item number two on the list); reduced taxation of pension plans (items three and five) and rapid depreciation for investment spending (item number 8). All these provisions in the tax code are very popular and would be very difficult to change. As we have discussed, in our current legal environment, it is difficult to tax capital gains at rates comparable to ordinary income. Reduced taxation for savings for retirement has strong bipartisan support, and there is typically strong support for encouraging business investment.

In Chapter 3, we explore whether and how capital income should be taxed and consider whether it would be better to partly exclude capital income and the returns from saving from taxation. This would move the tax system in the direction of taxing consumption rather than income. If we measured tax expenditures using a baseline of consumption taxation rather than income taxation, the reduced rates of taxation on capital gains and pensions and the rapid depreciation of investments would no longer be counted as tax expenditures.

Items four and seven are tax credits for children and other dependents, and the Earned Income Tax Credit. Both are already structured as credits, not deductions, and both aim to improve the life of lower-income families and wage earners. Child care credits have been expanded in recent years, and the Earned Income Tax Credit—effectively a wage subsidy—is supported by both political parties as an effective anti-poverty tool.

Item number six is the reduced tax rate on foreign business income earned through subsidiaries of U.S, multinationals. While this is certainly a tax expenditure because of the lower tax rate, Congress has always provided a lower rate for active foreign businesses to allow U.S.-owned businesses to compete more easily with foreign businesses that often have lower tax burdens. Another way to think of this tax preference is that foreign income earned by U.S. multinationals is to some degree elastic or sensitive to tax rates, so from an efficiency point of view, lower tax rates may be desirable.

Finally, at number ten, we have deductions for charitable contributions. There is much to criticize about our current policy. It provides a deduction, not a credit, so that it generates an upside-down subsidy. Our definition for what constitutes a charitable contribution is quite broad and encompasses many activities (such as semiprivate art galleries) that have limited public benefits. And, in violation of traditional tax policy principles, when donations are made of appreciated property—think of a painting that rose in value—the donor can deduct the full market value but avoid paying any capital gains taxes. Quite a subsidy for the rich! In its favor, however, is the long tradition of private philanthropy in the United States that predates the growth of the modern income tax and the general feeling that decisions about what types of charitable activities to support should primarily be in private hands, not those of the government. Providing charitable deductions allows individual taxpayers to make these decisions. Finally, we reviewed evidence that charitable contributions were very sensitive to tax rates.

After reviewing the top ten tax expenditures, we can conclude that they are either in the tax code for important political reasons—employer provided health exclusion, the Earned Income Tax Credit, charitable contributions; for efficiency reasons—lower rates for foreign income of U.S. multinationals; or reflect different views of how savings and income from capital should be taxed—capital gains preferences, preferences for pension contributions, rapid depreciation of investment assets. Trying to slash these top ten expenditures to lower tax rates would raise challenging political, philosophical and economic issues. No easy pickings, at least in the top ten.

Two well-known tax expenditures did not make our top ten: the mortgage interest deduction and the state and local tax deduction. The latter was capped at $10,000 in the 2017 tax act, moving it out of its previous top ten standing. In addition to limiting this specific deduction, the $10,000 cap had the effect, along with the increase in the standard deduction that was part of the 2017 act, of reducing the number of taxpayers who itemize on their returns. Consequently, fewer taxpayers claimed the mortgage interest deduction. Taxpayers who now claim the mortgage interest deduction have on average higher incomes than before; this suggests that it may now be a more opportune time for tax reformers to aim to eliminate the deduction entirely.

In its latest tax expenditure report, the U.S. Treasury listed 165 distinct tax expenditures.[25] Many could be targets for reformers. Not all of them would meet a stringent efficiency criterion to remain in the tax code. Nor do all reflect contested views about whether capital income and the returns to savings should be taxed. Tax reformers can rely on this list and a similar one developed by the Joint Committee on Taxation to determine if the listed expenditures are worthy of the political fight.

The Treasury, for example, lists charitable contributions to educational institutions as a tax expenditure. Any time an expenditure is listed, it poses some interesting questions. Would contributions to educational institutions decrease sharply if the charitable deduction were curtailed? Are the beneficiaries of this deduction predominantly the richest private educational institutions in the country or are they widely dispersed? Do they affect the educational fortunes of a wide range of students and parents or are they much more limited in scope? And going further afield, should the earnings of the endowments of the richest educational institutions be subject to some tax—as under current law since 2017?

All of these are legitimate questions. A tax expenditure budget is a useful tool for bringing these subsidies into the open so politicians of all stripes, reformers and interested citizens can now access them easily on their computers.

But simply calling something a tax expenditure does not mean it should be eliminated to broaden the base and lower the rates. Economic efficiency issues are important in the design of the tax system, and we may want lower rates or subsidies for certain types of incomes or activities and higher rates for others. Politicians and the public will certainly debate whether the alleged efficiencies of a given tax expenditure are real or simply self-serving justifications for favored treatment. There will be ongoing debates on whether a particular tax expenditure provides an important service that cannot be more appropriately supplied in other ways. Reformers should continue to probe the wisdom of tax expenditures, knowing that eliminating unnecessary ones can lead to lower rates or additional revenue. But there should be no illusion that a wholesale attack on tax expenditures is good tax policy.

This chapter showed that the traditional tax reform mantra, broad base and low rates, has severe limitations. As we discussed, it often runs contrary to economic analysis and raises important administrative and legal issues. The controversies over tax reform are a good illustration of the underlying deeper substructures which generate our tax debates.

Notes

1 Birnbaum and Murray, *Showdown at Gucci Gulch*. For a more academic discussion of the TRA see McLure and Zodrow, "Treasury I and the Tax Reform Act of 1986."
2 Technically there was an income range where the marginal rate reached 33 percent, but average rates were less than 28 percent.
3 Graetz, "The Truth about Tax Reform."
4 Passive loss rules disallow net losses from passive (nonactive) investments from offsetting ordinary income, such as wages.
5 Reilly, "Wandering Tax Pro Remembers the Tax Reform Act of 1986."
6 Liebman, "Who are Ineligible EITC Recipients?"
7 See Chapter 1 in McCaffery, *The Oxford Introductions to U.S. Law: Income Tax Law.*
8 The idea that higher rates can lead to lower revenues is colloquially known as the "Laffer curve."
9 The Urban Brookings Tax Policy Center uses a model in which the revenue maximizing capital gains rate is about 28 percent which is consistent with the revenue maximizing rate used by revenue estimators from Joint Committee on Taxation. See McClelland, "A New Study Suggests Congress Could Raise Money By Increasing Capital Gains Rate to 47 Percent: But There is a Catch." Other scholars, however, argue in favor of higher rates. See, for example, Agersnap and Zidar, "The Tax Elasticity of Capital Gains and Revenue Maximizing Rates."
10 Birnbaum, "Showdown at Gucci Gulch."
11 As quoted in Graetz, "The Truth about Tax Reform," 618.
12 Ibid.
13 There is a YouTube video that shows footage from 1978 of Milton Friedman articulating this view. Friedman, "Why Tax Reform is Impossible."
14 Hettich and Winer, *Democratic Choice, and Taxation.*
15 Friedman, "Tax Reform Lets Politicians Look for New Donors."
16 Ibid.
17 See Sheffrin, *The Making of Economic Policy*, Chapter 7.
18 Here and throughout the remainder of the chapter, I draw on the discussion in Hines, "High Tax Heresy."
19 Bakija, "Tax Policy and Philanthropy: A Primer on the Empirical Evidence for the United States and Its Implications," 557–84.
20 Hines, "High Tax Heresy."
21 Alm, "Is the Haig–Simons Standard Dead? The Uneasy Case for a Comprehensive Income Tax."

22 If someone were working, the first hour of leisure might be valued at the market wage, but what about the second or third? And, if someone was not working, what value would be used?

23 The Joint Committee on Taxation, however, does not count imputed income in its measures of untaxed income because they view this as impractical.

24 Tax Policy Center, "What are the Largest Tax Expenditures?"

25 U.S. Department of Treasury, Tax Expenditures. Fiscal Year 2023.

Chapter 3

SHOULD WE TAX INCOME
OR CONSUMPTION?

In November 2005, the President's Advisory Panel on Federal Tax Reform issued its report entitled *Simple, Fair, and Pro-Growth: Proposals to Fix America's Tax System*. The plural in "Proposals" was deliberate: the distinguished panel proposed two different tax proposals. The first, the Simplified Income Tax Plan, was a conventional reform of the income tax—broadening the base, lowering rates and making important suggestions for simplifying the application and administration of the income tax. The second, the Growth and Investment Tax Plan, was of a different nature—it was designed to be a consumption tax. The panel wanted to have a consumption tax alternative because of the general belief that taxing consumption was more favorable to economic growth than taxing income.

How does an income tax differ from a consumption tax? As the report explained in simplified terms, "The key difference between an income tax and a consumption tax is the tax burden on capital income. An income tax includes capital income in the tax base, while a consumption tax does not."[1] Another stylized way to explain the difference is that under a consumption tax, the return to savings will not be taxed. If an individual purchases a bond and receives interest, receives a dividend or earns a capital gain from investments in stocks, the interest, dividend or capital gain will not be subject to tax. Since income that is earned is either saved or consumed, removing taxes on savings means that any taxes will fall on consumption. Thus, exempting capital income (interest, dividends and capital gains) from individual tax returns will automatically tax consumption.[2]

There are many ways to tax consumption. The Growth and Investment Tax Plan developed a sophisticated approach to taxing consumption that preserved the progressivity of the tax, ensuring that the share of taxes paid rose as income increased. A conventional U.S. sales tax or a European style value-added tax does not have that property. For these types of familiar consumption taxes, the share of taxes paid does not rise with income—in fact, it falls, as lower-income households consume a higher fraction of income than higher income households. The Growth and Investment Tax Plan avoided that problem. It did so by imposing the consumption tax at both the business and individual or household level so that it could be tailored to individual or household circumstances.

A Puzzle

However, the plan had one feature that did not easily fit with the ideal of a consumption tax. It imposed a tax of 15 percent on interest, dividends and capital gains received by households. Here is the puzzle: Doesn't a consumption tax avoid taxing capital income? What drove the Advisory Panel to fail to recommend a pure consumption tax?

As we explain later in the chapter, economic theory suggests that consumption taxation might be superior to income taxation in terms of economic efficiency. But considerations of fairness, the psychology of public perceptions of taxation and administrative issues all make it difficult to implement an ideal consumption tax. Instead, the United States and other countries around the globe neither have a pure income tax or a pure consumption tax.

We instead have a hybrid system—part income tax, part consumption tax. While we officially claim we have an income tax in the United States, we tilt in the direction of a consumption tax in many ways. Here are the major ones: we tax capital gains at a lower rate than ordinary income and only when the gains are realized and never upon death; dividends are also taxed at lower rates than ordinary income; we provide a vast array of incentives for pensions and for retirement savings that effectively exempt them from substantial amounts of taxation and we allow businesses to deduct a substantial amount of their investments in the first or first few years they occur, rather than only allowing them deductions as their investments are subject to wear and tear. In addition to these major tilts toward exempting capital income, there are other important provisions in the tax code that have the same effect, such as favorable treatment for earnings from life insurance or for saving for college.

From the perspective of an income tax, all these programs are tax expenditures—deviations from an ideal income tax. In addition, you may recall many of these were the major ones on our top-ten list of tax expenditures that we highlighted in Chapter 2. Savings incentives are popular, and many are deeply embedded in our tax system. That is one reason the President's Advisory Panel wanted to see how far we could go in promoting a consumption tax.

It was not just a twenty-first century panel recommending consumption taxation. The idea has a long and distinguished pedigree. Thomas Hobbes in the *Leviathan* advocated for taxes on consumption rather than income, as consumption was a better measure of the protection one received from the state.[3] During World War II, the Treasury put forward a proposal for a progressive consumption tax to both raise revenue and curb consumption to fight inflation. As tax historian Joseph Thorndike described, the sophisticated tax proposal was based on previous plans developed by Treasury officials but met a quick death when it was presented to Congress.[4] It was not designed, however, to replace the income tax, but as a supplement to the income tax to raise revenue.

The modern revival of the consumption tax came in the 1950s from a British economist, Nicholas Kaldor, and in the 1970s by a Harvard law professor, William Andrews, both of whom recommended a progressive tax on consumption by removing savings from the tax base. By the late-1970s, consumption tax proposals made it into official government documents in the United Kingdom and the United States. In the United Kingdom, these ideas surfaced in the Meade Report in 1978.[5] In the United States, at the very end of the presidency of Gerald Ford in January 1977, the U.S. Treasury released a tax reform study, *Blueprints for Basic Tax Reform*, which again contained two proposals—one for an enhanced income tax and the other for a consumption tax.[6] The principal author of the proposal was Princeton economist David Bradford who was an intellectual leader in this field.

The tradition continued during the presidency of Ronald Reagan when the Secretary of the Treasury, Donald Regan, had his staff begin working on major tax reform. The resulting project *Tax Reform for Fairness, Simplicity and Economic Growth*, but known informally as Treasury I, actually discussed four plans—a flat tax, a modified flat tax, a consumed income tax (in the spirit of the *Blueprints*) and a sales tax.[7] But the modified flat tax (which the report ultimately recommended) and the consumed income tax were the two serious proposals. Between the *Blueprints* and Treasury 1, tax scholars at the Brookings Institution regularly debated the merits of consumption versus income taxation, working out many, but far from all, of the complicated theoretical and practical issues regarding the consumption tax.[8]

Further theoretical developments of the relative merits of consumption versus income taxation continued in the mid-1980s and strongly influenced thinking in the legal and economic community. We now turn to these developments which clarify the debate. As we will see, while the theoretical work favors consumption taxation, no real progress has been made on its implementation in the messy world of politics and policy. As a result, we continue in our hybrid limbo.

Types of Income and Consumption Taxation

In this section, we will discuss the several types of consumption taxes. But let us start with what they all have in common. All consumption taxes depart in one important way from the baseline income tax. Under an income tax, wages—including other forms of compensation such as fringe benefits—are subject to tax. In addition, capital income is also subject to the income tax. Capital income for individuals would consist of interest, dividends and capital gains. Under the Haig–Simon definition of income that we discussed in prior chapters, capital gains would include those not only realized (from sales) but also unrealized gains from the appreciation of financial assets.

To fix ideas and understand different methods to tax consumption, let us look at both the <u>sources</u> of income and the <u>uses</u> of income, which can be summarized in simple identities:

$$\text{Wages} + \text{Capital Income} = \text{Total Income} = \text{Consumption} + \text{Savings}$$

The left-hand identity just states that total income is equal to the income derived from wages and capital income. The right-hand identity states that total income can either be consumed or saved. This identity defines savings as whatever part of income is not consumed. With these identities in mind, let us see how several types of consumption taxes can arise.

Wage tax

Start with the identity on the left. Suppose we just taxed wage income but not capital income. Think of this as just omitting all forms of capital income from a conventional tax return. Since capital income is not included in the tax return, it is not subject to tax. What is surprising is that, under some simple assumptions, wage taxation is equivalent to taxing only consumption.

Consider a simple example. Suppose a young woman works in period 1 to consume in period 2. Specifically, let us assume she earns $100 of wage income in period 1, the tax rate is 20 percent, and the interest rate available to her for saving is 10 percent. After paying the wage tax, she has $80 remaining. She saves all of that for the second period.[9] Her savings earns her $8 of interest ($80 x 10 percent) but is not subject to tax under the wage tax. In the next period, she will then have $88 for consumption.

Now compare that to a tax on consumption of 20 percent. In the first period, she continues to save all her earnings, so she does not consume and therefore pays no tax. Her $100 is saved and earns $10 in interest for a total of $110. When she consumes the $110, she must pay a tax of $22 ($110 x

20 percent). She then has $(110–22) = $88 left over for consumption—the same amount as she had left with the wage tax. In this simple example, with a flat rate of tax, wage taxes are equivalent to taxes on consumption.[10]

To understand a bit more about wage taxation, assume that our young woman invests in a stock which then earns extraordinary returns—say 100 percent rather than just 10 percent. Since we are only taxing wages, the government will tax none of those extraordinary returns. Similarly, if the stock generates a zero return or even a negative return, the government does not refund her any of her loss. By paying the wage tax upfront, she prepaid her tax to the government. Windfall gains or losses accrue totally to the individual and not to the government.

One of the savings incentives in the United States works precisely like this. With a Roth Individual Retirement Account (IRA), an individual pays taxes on wage income and deposits the after-tax income into an account. The earnings are tax-free, and no further payment is due on withdrawing funds from the account. These accounts were originally designed to encourage retirement savings and limits were placed on eligibility and the amounts deposited into the accounts. But contrary to expectations, a few shrewd investors managed to open small accounts and purchased shares of speculative start-up stocks, initially worth little. When those stocks later exploded in value, the returns belonged exclusively to the investors, with no further tax ever due on the massive windfall gains.[11] That is how prepaid consumption taxes work.

A consumed income tax

Now let us look at the right-hand side of the identity. Since income equals consumption plus savings, if we remove savings from the tax base then all that is left is consumption. This is the strategy that was recommended by Nicholas Kaldor and William Andrews for taxing consumption. It is known as a consumed income tax.

To see how this works, consider our example of the young woman who worked in period 1 to consume in period 2. She earned $100 in period 1 and saved it all. Under a consumed income tax, her consumption subject to tax in period 1 is zero ($100 income – $100 savings). She earns a 10 percent return as before and has $110 available for consumption before tax in period 2. After paying the 20 percent consumption tax, she has $88 of consumption, just as before.

But suppose that instead of earning that boring 10 percent return, she invested in stocks and earned the extraordinary 100 percent return, so she now had $200 potentially available for consumption before tax. In period 2, she would pay $40 in tax, not $22 as before. The extra $18 in tax comes from her $90 in additional earnings from her stock investment. The government now does have an interest in her investment, sharing in the extraordinary gains. If the stock earned nothing and she only came into period 2 with $100, the government would tax her only $20, which is $2 less than before reflecting her reduced earnings. Under a consumed income tax, the government shares in windfall gains and losses. A consumed income tax is an example of a postpaid consumption tax.

There are two important examples of postpaid consumption tax ideas in U.S. tax law. The first is the conventional IRA in which any savings that are contributed to the account are deducted from income before taxes are applied. Therefore, if you contribute $100 to a conventional IRA and are in the 20 percent tax bracket, you immediately get a savings on your taxes of $20. Effectively the government has put up 20 percent of the account, and you only must contribute $80 net. Earnings accumulate tax free in the account, but when they are redeemed at retirement, the government includes *all* the proceeds, your initial contribution plus earnings and subjects them to the 20 percent tax. This has a nice logic to it: the government became a 20 percent (silent) partner with you up front and now wants its share back when funds are withdrawn from the account. This logic was the basis of the consumption tax proposals by Kaldor and Andrews, but they included all savings, not just specified retirement savings.

The second important example of postpaid consumption tax principles is a cash-flow corporation tax. Suppose that corporations are allowed to deduct the full amounts of their investments from their income before they calculate their taxes. This is known as expensing. Investment spending is treated like wages, supplies and everyday expenses so corporations can deduct their investments right away. This is equivalent to taxing the corporation on its cash flow from its real (not financial) activities.[12] If the corporation faces a tax rate of 30 percent, then a $1,000 investment will lead to an immediate tax savings of $300. The government becomes the silent partner of the corporation and taxes 30 percent of the later cash flow generated from the investment. Note that as a silent partner, the government shares in windfall gains or losses. If corporations make extraordinary returns on their investments, they share their good fortune with the government. More generally, under a postpaid consumption tax some capital income is taxed—the windfall component as well as possibly the returns that arise from risk bearing. The safe rate of return to investing, however, is not subject to tax.[13]

In summary, we have two types of consumption taxes: wage taxation or prepaid consumption taxes and consumed income taxation or postpaid consumption taxes. With these in mind, let us turn to the issue of the economic efficiency of consumption versus income taxes.

The Efficiency Argument for the Consumption Tax

To understand the modern economic arguments in favor of consumption tax-ation, it is useful to think of consumption at different dates as different com-modities—like luxury automobiles and designer watches. To make it simple, think of just two periods: consumption today and consumption in the future. Individuals allocate their lifetime resources between these two commodities. Savings is the way that current resources can be brought into the future to consume tomorrow. When a household saves, it reduces potential consump-tion now but increases it in the future.

As a basic principle, people attempt to smooth their consumption patterns over time, to maintain comparable consumption levels over time. This is pref-erable to starving today and feasting tomorrow or vice versa.[14]

This general principle is subject to two important qualifications. First, peo-ple do prefer, all else equal, to enjoy consumption today rather than later in the future. This is known as positive time preference. That would suggest that consumption would tilt more toward the present at the expense of the future. By itself, positive time preference would suggest more consumption today and less in the future.

But there is a factor working in the opposite direction—the cost of future consumption. Future consumption can be obtained more cheaply than con-sumption today because savings (which transform consumption today into consumption in the future) earn interest. With a 10 percent interest rate, $1 today becomes $1.10 tomorrow. Therefore, the "price" of one dollar of tomorrow's consumption in terms of today's consumption is $1/$1.10 or 0.91. Consumption tomorrow is 9 percent cheaper (1–0.91) than consump-tion today. The higher the interest rate, the cheaper consumption will be in the future. Since consumption tomorrow is cheaper than consumption today, individuals will take advantage of the lower price and tilt consumption toward the future.

If there were no taxes on savings—such as with a consumption tax—these two forces—time preference for the present and the cheaper cost of consump-tion in the future—would battle each other out. People would choose how much to consume today versus tomorrow based on their tastes and interest rates. Market outcomes would then determine consumption and savings behav-ior. Just as we let people choose between automobiles and luxury watches, we might be inclined to let people make their own choices about consumption and savings. Economists would say that with a consumption tax people's choices are efficient because they are not artificially distorted by taxation.

Enter the income tax. An income tax includes the return from savings in the tax base and reduces the return on savings. It therefore raises the price of future consumption distorting individual saving decisions. Relative to the market outcome, individuals now find that the cost of future consumption has risen and adjust their behavior accordingly. Normally, we would expect this to lead to lower savings, although that would depend on the individual preferences.[15] Regardless, behavior is distorted from the no-tax market outcome from a consumption tax.

Now as behavioral economists emphasize, individuals may have what they term an irrational present bias and a failure of imagination about the future that makes the market outcomes inefficient. Assume for the sake of argument that this is true. Even if you believe that people save too little, income taxation is not likely to be the right remedy. An income tax lowers the return to savings and, on balance, discourages savings.

Since savings takes place over prolonged periods of time, taxes on the returns to savings can potentially have exceptionally large effects. A 10 percent return will increase investment funds by a factor of 17.4 over a thirty-year horizon. With a 30 percent tax rate, the 10 percent return becomes 7 percent. This has major consequences. A $100 investment after thirty years would increase to $1745 with a 10 percent return, but only to $761 at a 7 percent after-tax return. The effects of compound interest over extended periods of time amplify or magnify the effects that the income tax has on lowering the rate of return to savings. Future consumption becomes more expensive over the long haul in the face of an income tax. It reduces the net returns to savings and distorts consumption and savings choices over time.

This magnification effect helps provide the intuition behind the influential work in the 1980s by Kenneth Judd and Christopher Chamley that provided theoretical models suggesting that the optimal tax rate on capital in the long run should be zero. This was true even in Judd's case when he considered the welfare of workers who earn only wages.[16] In his model, taxes on capital reduced capital accumulation so much through the magnification effect that it was best not to tax capital income at all.

One caveat to all the results for capital taxation is that at any point in time, returns from previously *existing* capital can be taxed efficiently. Since existing capital has already accumulated, there is no efficiency loss from even confiscating the returns from capital already in existence. One does not need to enact radical policies like the explicit confiscation of property. There are more subtle ways to tax the returns from prior investments. Consider our two examples of postpaid consumption taxes: cash flow corporate taxation and a consumed income tax. Suppose we switched from an income tax to cash flow taxation for firms while ignoring remaining depreciation deductions that firms were entitled to take under the income tax. This would tax the returns from the undepreciated existing capital. With respect to switching to a consumed income tax, suppose we now taxed all the proceeds of sales of stock that were not reinvested, while not allowing deductions for the previous after-tax investments that individuals had made in their stock holdings (the basis in their stock holdings). This policy would also tax the earnings from previously accumulated investments.

Whether and how to tax returns from existing capital is an important aspect in any proposed move to consumption taxation. Using models designed to mirror savings and investment behavior in actual economies, researchers have found that a significant fraction of the efficiency gains from switching from an income tax to a consumption tax largely arise because of the taxes levied on existing capital.[17] One of the reasons given for not adopting a consumed income tax in Treasury I were the complications, and potential unfairness, from taxing earnings from past capital ("old wealth") during the transition.[18] The Advisory Panel in 2005 also grappled with transitions issues for both of their plans, but stopped short of specific recommendations and instead advocated for a "transitional relief fund."[19]

Very recent academic scholarship has qualified some of the strongest Judd–Chamley results.[20] It turns out that both their theoretical models contained certain auxiliary assumptions that are needed to generate the zero long-run capital tax result. As one economist attempted to summarize this body of work, the result of a zero tax for capital income in the long run is not robust, but ideally you should tax capital "more today than tomorrow."[21] This is consistent with the intuition that existing capital should be taxed more than new capital.

Although the most refined theoretical models no longer suggest that zero capital taxation is always optimal in the long run, there is still a general acknowledgement of the efficiency argument for consumption taxation over income taxation. Why? Because income taxation can seriously distort the savings decisions individuals over how much to consume today versus in the future.

Will wage taxation work?

Opponents of consumption taxation worry about other issues especially the effects of consumption taxation on the distribution of income. We know that, on balance, the fraction of income that people save increases as their income increases. In other words, the share of consumption falls with income and the share of savings rises. The wealthy save more not just in total but also as a fraction of their income. Moving from an income tax that includes saving to a consumption tax that excludes savings will shift the burden from higher-income to lower-income individuals. How can we address this?

Let us start with a simple example outside the realm of the income-consumption tax debate. Suppose that we had a wage tax of 30 percent that applied equally to the rich and poor. As a society, we decide we want to spend more on government services but have the rich bear this extra burden of taxation. We notice that the rich consume luxury cars and decide to put an excise tax (a special sales tax) on the purchases of luxury cars. Since the rich continue to buy cars after we imposed the tax, we have successfully raised money for the government and shifted the tax burden to the rich.

But there is a better solution for raising revenue and shifting the burden of taxation. When we impose the excise tax on cars, we distort the choices that rich people make between cars, luxury vacations or other goods. We can figure out on average what the rich pay in excise taxes, remove the excise tax itself, but increase the tax rate on their wages to compensate for the removal of the excise tax. After this change, the rich would have a higher tax rate on wages than the poor. We would have redistributed the tax burden to the rich but avoided distorting the consumption choices of the rich. The rich should prefer this method and because they are better off; they might even be willing to transfer a bit more to the poor than before.

The same logic can be applied to income and consumption taxes. Under an income tax, savers have their choices distorted between consumption at different periods of time. If the rich save more and would normally benefit by switching from an income tax to a consumption tax, why not eliminate the taxation on savings but raise taxes on wages for the wealthy?

Table 3.1 provides a simple example of how this would work. In Table 3.1 we have three individuals: poor, middle and rich. The poor person earns 100, all of it is in wages. The middle-income person earns 200 of which 150 is wages (the remainder capital income), and the rich person earns 400 of which only 200 is wages. An income tax of 20 percent would raise (20, 40, and 80) from this group, while a 20 percent wage tax would raise (20, 30, and 40). Under a wage tax, the middle and rich person would pay less. But consider a progressive wage tax with rates (20 percent. 26.6 percent and 40 percent).

Table 3.1 Replacing an income tax with a progressive wage tax

	Poor	*Middle*	*Rich*
Income	100	200	400
Wages	100	150	200
Income Tax 20%	20	40	80
Wage Tax 20%	20	30	40
Progressive Wage Tax Rates	20%	26.6%	40%
Progressive Wage Tax Payments	20	40	80

The progressive wage tax would then replicate the original tax burden under the income tax and have the benefit that the savings decisions of the middle-income and rich person would not be distorted.

The key to this strategy is to adjust the wage tax for distributional purposes but avoid distorting individual decisions—whether they are between luxury cars and vacations or between consumption today and consumption in the future. The original insight for this idea came from theoretical work in public finance in the late 1970s from Anthony Atkinson and Joseph Stiglitz. Louis Kaplow used a similar approach to re-think public finance generally, while a number of sophisticated legal scholars, including David Weisbach and Joseph Bankman, brought these ideas to the legal academic community.[22] The economic theory behind this approach does rely on a few assumptions on individual preferences which imply that no additional economic distortions in decisions about how much to work (the labor-leisure choice) are created by shifting taxation from future consumption to current wages. Economists typically consider these assumptions to be reasonable.[23]

There is one obvious weakness to this approach to offset the adverse distributional consequences of consumption taxes. Continuing with our example, suppose that the rich person did not have any wage income at all—she simply lived off interest, dividends and capital gains. In that case, increasing the rate of wage taxation would not work—our rich person would still pay no tax. Wage taxation does not mean much for people who do not earn wages. This is the extreme case of the natural differences that may occur if savings behavior differs within wage groups. Not all rich people save the same percentage, so a progressive wage adjustment would not really differentiate among this group.

Not only would the progressive wage strategy not technically work for the rich who live off capital income, but it would appear patently unfair to the public. Many of the rich inherited their money so they would not be fairly taxed under such a scheme. But even if more rich people worked to achieve their fortunes, the system would still not strike the average citizen or taxpayer as fair. Older people, for example, are more likely to have a high percentage of capital income and this would generate the phenomenon of younger workers paying higher taxes, even with the same level of overall income. One could argue that over a lifetime this would balance out, but nonetheless it would constantly raise difficult comparisons. Shrewd investors, early employees of Amazon or Google, or purchasers of stocks with extraordinary gains would also be difficult to reach with wage taxation. But wage taxation is just one form of a consumption tax—effectively a prepaid tax. How about a consumed income tax or a postpaid consumption tax?

A consumed income tax solution?

In principle, a consumed income tax could satisfy many of our concerns. Proponents of consumed income taxes, such as legal scholar Edward McCaffery, have praised its virtues and suggested a progressive consumption tax.[24] Bill Gates, also agrees: "I think we'd be best off with a progressive tax on *consumption*."[25]

According to Gates, when we compare the poor, middle and rich, we should focus on how much they consume. The heir who lives off capital income will still want to purchase jewelry, travel on private jets, eat exorbitant meals and live in luxurious mansions or exclusive apartments in New York City. He will pay considerable amounts of tax. A more frugal heir with the same income who lived a more modest lifestyle would pay less tax. That is the consequence of any consumption-based tax, but the public would likely learn to perceive this as fair. Windfalls would be taxed once they are consumed in contrast to wage taxation. It might take some time before the public tunes its "fairness radar" to consumption as opposed to income as a standard of welfare, but such a transformation is potentially conceivable.

Even with a consumed income tax, there are some fundamentally difficult issues that must be addressed upfront. The first is inheritances or intergenerational transfers of wealth. When a wealthy person dies and passes on his or her fortune, should that be classified as "consumption" and subject to tax? One could argue that the wealthy person gains satisfaction from the bequest and so it should be considered as consumption. Others, though, would say that no taxes should be applied on bequests. Only when the heirs start spending their inherited fortunes on consumption goods should there be any taxation. This would be a major decision in the design of the tax, as it would have implications for actual wealth transfers and the size of estates.

A similar argument could be applied to charity. The charitable donor surely feels that his or her donation is worthwhile and gains satisfaction from it. Should that be considered consumption? Some tax theorists say no, because these gifts are directed to others—but others may disagree and include Bill Gates's gifts to his own foundation as consumption, especially since this may be a mixture of legacy building as well as pure charity.

Others may have a more fundamental objection to consumption taxes. Under a consumption tax, there is no tax applied to investment earnings, which means that wealth grows more rapidly than under an income tax. While allowing for wealth accumulation is one of the purposes of a consumption tax, it would lead to more wealth being accumulated, larger fortunes and even more wealth inequality. That may be objectionable. Wealth conveys status; wealth conveys power. Critics of our current income tax point out that the extraordinarily rich today often just accumulate their wealth through untaxed, unrealized capital gains. They view this as a problem with the current income tax system and suggest either some means to tax unrealized gains or even wealth taxes. Some politicians and economists advocate for wealth taxation that reduces fortunes explicitly as a social goal.[26]

The debate about whether the distribution of wealth matters and how it would evolve under our current income tax system, an ideal income tax system or an ideal or less than ideal consumption tax system is not easily settled. Since we do not have an ideal income tax or a consumption tax, there is no readily available empirical data to rely upon to settle this dispute.

However, uncertainties about the evolution of wealth are not the reason that we have never seen a comprehensive consumption tax replace the income tax in modern times. While we have major sales and value-added taxes, nowhere do they totally replace personal income taxes. The reason for this lies more in the mundane and practical realities of tax administration and human psychology than uncertainties about wealth accumulation.

Would a Comprehensive Consumption Tax Actually Work?

Advocates for a new system of taxation that departs from our current hybrid system face a high burden. This would certainly be true if the goal were to move the current system to a Haig–Simons ideal income tax, one in which all gains were taxed to individuals as they were accrued, whether those gains were realized or not. Since we have been reluctant since the inception of the income tax to move our tax system in this direction, there must have been formidable political and administrative barriers to such a transition.

Proponents of consumption taxes potentially face even a greater burden, as they must confront administrative issues as well as persuade the public that the returns from savings and capital income should be exempt from tax. Surprisingly though, proponents of consumption taxes have developed a variety of proposals to implement their vision. While I argue that these and similar proposals would not really work in the United States, we nonetheless can give tribute to their ingenuity and subtlety.

There are two basic types of consumption tax proposals that have been offered for practical consideration. The first model would be structured as a consumed income tax for households only, with no taxes levied on business enterprises. The second model relies on both households and businesses to implement the system.

Household-based consumption tax

Let us start with the household-only model, based on the scholarship of Kaldor and Andrews, and developed as a full-fledged proposal for the U.S. Treasury's 1977 *Blueprints for Basic Tax Reform*. Consumption tax proponents have emphasized that their proposals do not require complex measurements of income—such as accurate estimates of depreciation or inflation adjustments—that are required in an income tax. For some, this is the most compelling argument for a consumption tax.[27] In a consumption tax system, individuals would be taxed on their *cash flow* in any given year. The goal is to tax consumption by removing savings from the tax base.

How would this work? Individuals would first tally up their receipts from wages and sales of any assets. Then they would subtract any purchases of assets during the year. Borrowing is negative savings, so any proceeds from new loans would be included in the tax base, but repayments of the loan (including interest) would be subtracted. Net savings consists of the purchases of assets plus repayments of loans minus sales of assets and new borrowing. The net result from these adjustments is to remove net savings from the tax base and just leave consumption as the tax base.

To make this work, the government must keep track of net savings. In the 1977 *Blueprints* study, this is first accomplished through qualified accounts where individuals can buy and sell assets, borrow funds and repay them. These qualified accounts could be maintained by financial intermediaries, banks, corporations, brokerages or similar institutions. They would be responsible for reporting transactions to the government so that households would accurately report their net cash flow.

The *Blueprints* proposal however recognized that not all savings could be run through these qualified accounts. Consumer durables, such as housing, pose a problem. These are in effect investments (savings) so should be allowed as a deduction in any consumed income tax. However, the services provided by the durable (the rental equivalent of living in the house) are not monetized and could not easily be included in a calculation of cash flow. Allowing for a deduction for housing purchases but failing to include the value of housing services would provide a dramatic tax subsidy for households and a loss of revenue to the government. To deal with this problem, the plan in the *Blueprints* not only would not allow a deduction for the purchase of the house but also would not tax the services provided by housing. Consumer durables would thus lie outside of the qualified accounts.

The *Blueprints* also suggested that households should have the freedom to conduct at least some other financial transactions outside the qualified accounts as well. Suppose you took a mortgage to buy a house, and the mortgage was in a qualified account. Since the mortgage is new borrowing, it would be included fully in your current year cash flow—subjecting your household to a substantial tax increase. Many years later when the mortgage is paid off, your household would experience a sharp drop in cash flow. To avoid these dramatic swings in cash flow, mortgage funds could be borrowed outside a qualified account with neither the borrowing nor repayment affecting the tax base. What about the down payment for the house? If the funds were withdrawn from a qualified account, the household would pay tax on the added cash flow. To avoid this, the household would have had to have the foresight to accumulate the down payment outside a qualified account.

On the other hand, if funds were routinely accumulated outside of qualified account, this would allow individuals who made large fortunes to escape tax—just as with a Roth IRA. To avoid this problem, the *Blueprints* suggested limits on what types of assets could be allowed outside of qualified accounts. But clearly this would add considerable complications and complexity for the cash flow household model and potentially would be unworkable.

Two other features of the household consumption tax raise difficult political and public perception issues. Under the cash flow tax, all borrowing is included in the tax base and subject to tax. But while borrowing does increase cash flow, it is not income as normally conceived. The idea of being taxed on borrowing would seem alien to most people. Even tax scholars who favor consumption taxes have seen this perception issue as the key weakness of the household consumption tax.[28]

The second perception issue is that there are no taxes on businesses or on corporations. The public sees corporations as an important source of economic power and wants them to pay tax. There is also a long history of taxing corporations. The first corporate tax in the United States was enacted in 1909, before the individual income tax in 1913. At the state level, corporate taxes were enacted along with individual income taxes.

All told, the strangeness of including borrowing in the tax base, the absence of corporations from the tax system, and the difficulties in creating a system to manage savings and dissaving for households are just some of the complex political and administrative issues that would arise with replacing the income tax with a household consumption tax. But could another model work?

Business-household consumption tax

In 1981, Robert Hall and Alvin Rabushka introduced the flat tax in an op-ed in the *Wall Street Journal* and published a short book describing their proposal in 1985.[29] At the time, the excitement surrounding the book centered on both its simplicity for individual and business filing and the fact that there was a single flat rate of 19 percent for both business and individuals. But the true novelty of the proposal was that it provided a framework for a business-household consumption tax that later scholars and tax reform commissions refined.

The flat tax imposed a cash flow tax on business allowing a full deduction for ordinary expenses, purchases of investment goods and wages. Aside from the deduction for wages, it is the same as a value-added tax. Wages are included in household returns which would allow an amount to be exempt from tax to provide some progressivity to the tax system. Individuals do not include dividends, interest or capital gains on their tax returns—the rationale for this omission is that the earnings of the business are taxed so there is no need to tax them again on the individual return.

Subsequent tax reform proposals were built on the Hall–Rabushka framework. In a 1986 book, David Bradford discusses several different versions of these types of taxes.[30] Once wages are deducted at the business level and taxed at the household level, it is possible to have a full schedule of tax rates and increase the progressivity of the tax system even further. An important feature of all these proposals is that extraordinary economic returns on investments are taxed at the business level. When businesses expense their investment, the government becomes a silent partner and shares in any extraordinary returns. There is no need to have a separate tax on the capital income of individuals to reach these extraordinary returns. Unlike the household-only consumption tax model, there is no need for households to include borrowing to calculate their taxes. In this model, businesses remit taxes as well as individuals, potentially solving a perception problem for the consumption tax.

There are, of course, complex administrative issues that emerge with these types of taxes as well. It is difficult to design a system based on real cash flows to tax financial institutions, particularly when financial flows—their reason for existence—are ignored in the tax calculation. There are also complex issues with international taxation, in particular which international transactions are subject to tax.[31] The Advisory Panel did attempt to deal with these issues directly and offered their own solutions.

Puzzle Resolved?

The Growth and Investment Plan from the 2005 President's Advisory Panel on Tax Reform was designed as a business-household consumption tax. Businesses were taxed on a cash flow basis, and wages were subject to progressive tax rates at the household level. But unlike the prototype flat tax, capital income was subject to tax at the individual level. Some members of the panel did not wish to have a household-level tax on capital income and suggested an alternative without it. They called this alternative the Progressive Consumption Plan. It eliminated the 15 percent tax at the household level for capital income and made up the revenue by imposing slightly higher rates for wage and business income. But the Advisory Panel did not choose this alternative.

Why did the Advisory Panel reject the Progressive Consumption Plan? By their own estimates, it would produce higher long-term growth than the Growth and Investment Plan and allocate capital more efficiently. It would also avoid having households keep detailed records on financial transactions. The principal reason they offered for not choosing this alternative was that the distribution of the tax burden was less progressive than under the Growth and Investment Plan. But a close look at their own figures in the report indicate that the differences were very minor—certainly within the margin of error for estimating distributional burdens.[32]

A better clue to the underlying motivation came from their discussion of how the tax burden would be *perceived* under the two systems. Since the Progressive Tax Plan had a higher rate, more of the windfall gains from investing would be taxed at the corporate level. They note that this "tax burden on business reduces the amount that the firm is able to pay in dividends to shareholders, but the shareholder does not write a check to the government and so does not *appear* to make a tax payment."[33] (Italics in original) Here the Commission tipped its hand. The perception of who pays taxes matters; not having the rich remit taxes is a political perception problem, even if rich still bear the tax burden.

Moreover, there is a key transition issue that goes beyond appearances. Without a tax on capital income at the household level, returns from preexisting investments held in personal portfolios outside of businesses would not be subject to tax. That would mean that wealthy individuals would be able to enjoy the fruits from past investments without paying any taxes.

The Advisory Panel judged that the Progressive Consumption Plan would not stand politically (and possibly did not meet their own personal standards of perceived fairness) so put forward a workable compromise. Like many compromises, it satisfied no one—pure consumption tax advocates found the proposal to be just another mixed system with "an appended, ill-fitting 15 percent tax," while income tax advocates would point to the inequities of a lower rate on capital income than on wage income.[34]

In recent years, the political mood in the United States has swung more in the direction of income taxation with a focus on accumulated wealth and the unrealized capital gains of billionaires. Emmanuel Saez and Gabriel Zucman express the modern-day skepticism toward consumption taxation: "The fundamental injustice of consumption taxes, relative to income taxes, is that the well-off can postpone them by saving, while the poor pay cash on the nail."[35] The political moment is not ripe for a wholesale replacement of an income tax by a consumption tax.

But this debate is not over. There is a long-run need for an additional revenue source to meet future challenges for an aging society, climate change and other national priorities. Ever-growing government deficits are not sustainable. To meet these needs, the United States will also need to increase its stock of capital to ensure economic growth. This opens the possibility for additional consumption taxation which would not burden the return to savings.

The consumption tax debate illustrates the full range of underlying factors that drive tax policy controversies. Distributional issues do initially dominate the debate, as consumption taxes are often seen as unfair. But behind the distributional debate lie considerations of economic efficiency, the psychology of taxation and complex administrative issues which weigh heavily on the possibility of designing efficient and politically palatable consumption taxes.

Notes

1 President's Advisory Panel on Federal Tax Reform, *Simple, Fair and Pro-Growth*, 152.
2 As we discuss later in the chapter, there are several types of consumption taxes, some of which tax some component of capital income.
3 Metcalf, "Consumption Taxation," in *Encyclopedia of Taxation and Tax Policy*, 74.
4 Thorndike, "Comment," 153–62.
5 Meade, ed., *The Structure and Reform of Direct Taxation*.
6 U. S. Dept. of Treasury, *Blueprints for Basic Tax Reform*.
7 U.S. Dept. of Treasury, *Tax Reform for Fairness, Simplicity, and Economic Growth*.
8 Pechman, ed., *What Should Be Taxed: Income or Expenditure?*
9 The fact that she saves all the income is just illustrative and does not affect the basic argument.
10 This result only holds for a proportional wage tax. Some scholars have advocated for progressive consumption taxes.
11 Some actual cases are discussed in Elliott et al., "Lord of the Roths: How Tech Mogul Peter Theil Turned a Retirement Account for the Middle Class Into a $5 Billion Tax-Free Piggy Bank."
12 It is possible to design a tax that includes financial flows as well as real flows.
13 Economists distinguish between different types of returns to investing. The return to an investment can be broken down into a safe rate of return, a risk premium for undertaking a risky investment, and any windfall gains or losses. Under a postpaid consumption tax, windfall returns are always subject to tax while the safe rate of return in not. Whether the risk premium is also subject to tax depends on the underlying economic assumptions.
14 We are abstracting here from cases in which the individual may want to borrow against future income. Taxing capital income, however, does not make this any easier.
15 It is possible in theory that by making individuals poorer through taxing savings that savings could increase. But that is viewed as a less likely outcome.
16 See Judd, "Redistributive Taxes in a Simple Perfect Foresight Model," and Chamley, "Optimal Taxation of Capital Income in General Equilibrium with Infinite Lives."
17 See Altig et al., "Simulating Fundamental Tax Reform In the United States."
18 U.S. Dept. of Treasury, *Tax Reform for Fairness, Simplicity, and Economic Growth*, 210.
19 See Poterba, "The Recommendations of the President's Advisory Panel on Federal Tax Reform: A Two-Year Retrospective."

20 Straub and Werning, "Positive Long-Run Capital Taxation: Chamley-Judd Revisited." The authors show that the results of Judd and Chamley depend intimately on the assumptions underlying the models. For example, in the Judd model if consumption is not easily substitutable over time, then rising tax rates will lead to more savings, build up the capital stock, and sustain a positive rate of capital taxation even in the long run.

21 Moll, Princeton Lecture 8, "Policy Analysis in a Growth Model."

22 See Atkinson-Stiglitz, "The Design of Tax Structure: Direct versus Indirect Taxation," Kaplow, *The Theory of Taxation and Public Economics*, and Bankman and Weisbach, "The Superiority of an Ideal Consumption Tax over an Ideal Income Tax."

23 The theory relies on an idea of separability between decisions to supply labor and consumption. More specifically, for any given level of labor supply, the trade-off between consumption today and consumption in the future just depends on the cost of future consumption relative to consumption today and not the level of labor supply.

24 McCaffery, "A New Understanding of Tax."

25 Gates, "Why Inequality Matters."

26 See Saez and Zucman, *The Triumph of Injustice*.

27 See Bradford, *Untangling the Income Tax*.

28 Shaviro, "How Might the Politics of Consumption Tax Reform Affect (Impair) the End Product?"

29 See Hall and Rabushka, "A Proposal to Simplify Our Tax System," and *The Flat Tax*.

30 See the discussion of the X tax in Bradford, *Untangling the Income Tax*.

31 The key international issue is whether taxes are levied on a destination basis or a source basis. Under a destination tax, like the traditional VAT, imports are taxed but exports are exempt from taxation. This is reversed under a source basis.

32 Under the Growth and Investment Plan the top quintile would pay 84.1 percent of the tax burden (Figure 7.4, p. 175) while the corresponding percent for the Progressive Consumption Tax Plan would be 83.8 (Figure 7.11, p. 185), a difference of only 0.3 percentage points. There were slightly larger differences for the top 1 percent. The Panel did not elaborate on these distributional differences in any detail in the text of their report.

33 President's Advisory Panel on Federal Tax Reform, *Simple, Fair and Pro-Growth*, 185.

34 See Shaviro, "How Might the Politics of Consumption Tax Reform Affect (Impair) the End Product?" 81.

35 Saez and Zucman, *The Triumph of Injustice*, 186.

Chapter 4

DO WE NEED A NEW SYSTEM TO TAX MULTINATIONAL CORPORATIONS?

In the last decade, there have been a series of dramatic changes in the system for taxing multinational corporations and international income, a system that had originally been put in place in the 1920s. A series of factors—increasing globalization of economic activity, the changing nature of multinational corporation from manufacturing or resource giants to purveyors of digital technology and knowledge and aggressive behavior by both firms and countries to take advantage of the old system—all have led to whirlwind change. Why precisely did the international tax system seem to break down and where is it now headed?

The story begins in the aftermath of the 2009 financial crisis and the worldwide recession that forced many governments, especially in Europe, into policies of fiscal austerity. At that time reports began to surface in the press about the elaborate and byzantine strategies that multinational corporations were using to reduce their own taxes. As recounted in Chapter 1, these and other revelations soon led to U.S. Senate and U.K. Parliamentary hearings, furthering a climate of outrage against these aggressive tax practices.

Perhaps the most famous of these was the Double-Dutch Sandwich. While a full explanation of this tax strategy would require an advanced course in international tax law, the idea behind it can be grasped intuitively.[1] Google transferred its intellectual property to an Irish subsidiary to service the market in Europe and the Middle East. For U.S. tax purposes, this subsidiary was an Irish company as it was incorporated there, but Ireland considered it a Bermuda-based company because it was ostensibly managed from there. The Irish company re-licensed the intellectual property to a newly created Dutch company which, in turn, re-licensed it to a second, newly created Irish company, which managed the intellectual property. Royalty payments flowed out of European and the Middle Eastern countries to the second Irish company, on to the Dutch company, and eventually back to the original Irish subsidiary. Through the intricacies of Irish, United States and Dutch tax law and careful tax planning, the royalty payments eventually ended up primarily being subject to tax in Bermuda. Through these machinations, Google was able to reduce the tax rate on the income it earned from Europe and the Middle East to 2.4 percent.[2]

At that time under U.S. tax law, no U.S. tax was due on Google's earnings abroad if the funds were not sent back to the United States. If they were brought back, however, they would have faced a U.S. tax rate of 35 percent, with a credit provided for any foreign taxes Google had paid. But Google did not want to repatriate any funds back to the United States and kept its foreign taxes low through this and other strategies. As a result, by 2017, Google and many other multinational corporations had accumulated trillions of dollars in funds overseas.[3] If these companies needed cash for their U.S. operations or to pay dividends to shareholders, they could and sometimes did borrow using the overseas funds as collateral.

The European countries disliked having their tax base depleted through royalty payments, while the U.S. government did not like the extra borrowing the companies did because it reduced U.S. taxable income. The United States especially disliked those trillions of dollars being held abroad, out of the reach of the tax authorities. Politicians and the public understood just enough to know that these tax strategies were unseemly.

Three Dramatic Responses

Something had to change, and the responses moved forward in three acts. The first major step was taken by the Organization for Economic Co-operation and Development (OECD) through their Base Erosion and Profit Shifting (BEPS) project. The original BEPS project, which began in 2013 and continued for several years, was designed to prevent corporate profits from being shifted from high-tax jurisdictions (such as Germany) to low-tax jurisdictions (such as Bermuda).[4] It focused primarily on eliminating "tax mismatches" which were used to shift profits from one country to another. For example, a payment from company 1 in Country A to company 2 in Country B might be characterized as deductible interest for company 1 but as nontaxable dividends received by company 2. As a result, income was removed from the tax base of Country A but was not taxed in Country B. Consequently, the income was taxed nowhere.

Above all, the BEPS project wanted to pressure Ireland and other countries to change their rules so that the complex strategies like the Double-Dutch sandwich would no longer be feasible. The project was generally successful in eliminating the most egregious abuses.

The second step in the process was taken by the United States in the 2017 tax legislation. The new law ended the ability of U.S. companies to simply keep their foreign earnings overseas and avoid all taxes. The new law taxed the previously accumulated funds held overseas at a lower rate, which immediately brought some revenue to the U.S. Treasury and enabled U.S. companies to repatriate the funds without further penalty. Going forward, it put in a new tax on foreign earnings of U.S. companies known as Global Intangible Low Taxed Income (GILTI). GILTI effectively placed a minimum tax on multinational corporations on any foreign income earned through overseas subsidiaries over and above a baseline return to investment. This reduced the incentives to shift profits to low-tax countries.

The third step was then taken by the OECD countries who now wanted to go beyond their previous BEPS initiatives to deal with two problems that they believed still plagued the international tax system. The OECD decided it needed broader political support and brought in more than 130 countries (known as the Inclusive Framework) to develop a new legal framework in two different areas.

One initiative was aimed at curbing tax competition. Inspired by the U.S. GILTI tax, they proposed that all countries have a minimum tax. If, for example, Bermuda, Ireland, the Netherlands, Singapore, or another low-tax country did not impose a high enough tax, the parent country of the multinational corporation whose subsidiaries were operating in those low-tax countries would be required to "top-up" the tax to reach some minimum. If all major countries had these top-up taxes there would be reduced incentives for multinationals to set up operations or shift profits to low-tax countries simply to reap tax advantages. This legal framework—known as Pillar 2—was effectively a cartel agreement among countries to keep tax rates high. No longer was the focus solely on profit-shifting; the desire was to prevent all countries from competing based on taxes, even for real activity.

The other initiative—known as Pillar 1—focused on the reality that large web-based digital companies such as Google or Facebook (now Meta) were earning profits throughout the world but paying little tax in many of those countries. The reason they paid so little tax was that they had minimal physical presence and thus had not created a permanent establishment in those countries. Under conventional international tax law, a foreign corporation must have set up a permanent establishment—a physical locus of economic activity—in a country before that country can impose a tax on its operations. The large digital companies carefully avoided being subject to tax in many countries where they provided profitable services to the population.

Frustrated by this inability to tax the major digital companies, many countries, including the United Kingdom, France, Spain, India and others, began to impose digital taxes on advertising or other web-based activities. The digital taxes typically were taxes on the revenues earned from advertising-related activities. The United States strongly opposed the digital taxes because they were perceived to be aimed solely at U.S. multinationals. The United States threatened to impose tariffs on countries that levied them. No one was happy with the status quo.

As a solution to this conundrum, the OECD developed the Pillar 1 framework, which would reallocate a fraction of the profits of the largest companies in the world to the countries in which corporations made sales. Under Pillar 1, 25 percent of the "excess profits" of the 100 or so largest nonfinancial multinationals would be reallocated to countries based on local sales. Excess profits would be defined as any profits that exceeded a value of 10 percent of total sales. As a result, some fraction of Facebook and Google's profits would be reallocated to countries based on the sales in those countries. As part of the Pillar 1 deal, countries would relinquish the ability to impose digital taxes.

The OECD Pillar 1 proposals is a radical reorientation of the international tax system because it would allocate or apportion profits to jurisdictions where sales were made without requiring physical presence as an indicator of substantial economic activity in that country. For years the OECD countries, including the United States, have resisted apportioning profits based on sales or other factors. Instead, the OECD has insisted on taxing profits based on the income that was presumed to be generated in each country through methods known as transfer pricing which attempt to assign income to each separate corporation.

The traditional transfer price-oriented approach advocated by the OECD was not without difficulties. Multinational corporations consist of complex webs of separately constituted individual corporations, so it is necessary to use transfer pricing methods (discussed in more detail below) to determine how much of the profit of the entire multinational is attributable to each company. In a partial break from this tradition, Pillar 1 would begin a process of jettisoning the traditional system and moving toward a system based on apportionment of corporate income.

In the face of such potentially radical change, it is important to step back and evaluate the proposed new program. There are three key questions that should be addressed. First, what is the rationale for taxing the profits of purely domestic or multinational corporations in the first place? Second, does the data suggest that the current system is truly in a crisis mode or is the current transfer pricing system evolving to produce more satisfactory outcomes on its own? Third, what would be the consequences of shifting to an entirely new system whereby we apportion the profits of the major multinational corporations?

Why Should We Tax Corporate Income?

Traditional rationales

The traditional rationale for taxing corporate income is to prevent individual taxpayers from using corporations as a tax shelter.[5] If corporate income were not taxed until it was distributed back to its owners, individuals could design their affairs to earn income within corporate structures and delay distributing profits from the corporation. As a simple example, individuals could conduct all their investment activities through corporations. If there were no corporate tax, and the earnings from investments remained within the corporation, there would be no taxes due until the owners decided to have the corporation either pay dividends or purchase some of the corporate stock from the shareholders. As a result, taxes due on the income that was earned through investments could be deferred far into the future. Taxes deferred are taxes reduced. Without a corporate tax, individuals could sharply reduce individual taxes on their earnings. A corporate tax, however, can prevent these deferral strategies, since the income earned within the corporation would be immediately subject to tax.

This rationale is powerful when corporations and shareholders are all located in the same country—what is typically known as the closed economy case. In this case, the corporate tax rate and the tax rates on any distributions from corporations could be set such to reduce any advantages to operating within the corporate sector as compared to making investments outside the corporate sector by using legal structures where the income is passed directly through to individuals without any corporate-level tax. These pass-through structures include partnerships, sole proprietorships and, in the U.S., S-corporations.

The idea that the corporate tax serves as a backstop to individual taxation also has great intuitive appeal because it emphasizes the association between corporate income and its shareholders. The income of the corporation belongs to its shareholders, and intuitively this income should be taxed as it is earned. The corporate tax accomplishes the current taxation of shareholder income, while allowing the corporation its prerogative to decide what portion of earnings to retain for its own investments or distribute them to their shareholders.

The backstop rationale for corporate taxation becomes more complicated when corporations operate internationally and in different locales from where their owners reside—the open economy case.[6] In open economy settings, there are two key complicating factors. First, countries like the United States typically want to tax the income of their domestic residents that are earned abroad. Second, they will also want to tax the income of both foreign and domestic companies that operate within their own country. These two features of open-economy taxations raise some difficulties with the backstop rationale for corporate taxation.

Let us consider a simple example. Suppose that a U.S. individual owns minority shares in an Indian corporation that actively operates a business in India.[7] Since the U.S. taxes its citizens on their worldwide income, the United States would like to tax the income of the Indian corporation attributable to the U.S. shareholder as it is earned. But it cannot easily do so because the income is earned in a foreign company and the U.S. government cannot directly tax it. The United States must wait until the foreign corporation pays dividends back to its U.S. shareholder before it can impose any tax. Therefore, there is no direct U.S. tax on the current earnings of the Indian company for that individual.

At the same time, the government of India will tax the profits of that corporation with its own corporate tax because the company is operating in India. There is no direct connection between the taxes levied on that corporation by the Indian government and the amount that the U.S. government would want to tax on the Indian earnings based on a backstop rationale. India will have full discretion to tax the income of that corporation at whatever rates it chooses. It could decide to impose a low rate of tax to attract investment to the country. In this case, the earnings of the corporation will be very lightly taxed, and the U.S. shareholder would face an overall low current tax burden. Or the India government might choose a high rate of taxation to raise domestic revenue. In this case, the U.S. resident may have a high current tax burden.

In this simple example, the Indian corporate tax serves as an imperfect backstop for individual taxation. The United States does not tax the current earnings of foreign corporations attributable to the individual. The Indian corporate tax does impose a current tax, but at a rate which is unrelated to U.S. tax rates, either corporate or individual. Perhaps by coincidence, the Indian tax would mirror the ideal U.S. tax on individuals on a current basis, but there is no reason why this would need to hold.

Alternative rationales

A populist rationale for taxing corporations is that they deserve to pay taxes on their income because they have an existence independent of their shareholders. Both legally and as a sociological fact, they are distinct from their owners. Under this entity view of taxation, corporations should pay taxes as should all entities that earn income. Shareholders may own corporations, but they operate as separate entities and should pay tax. Unlike the aggregative view which looks to the owners of the corporation and their tax burdens, the entity view focuses on the tax obligations of the corporation itself.

The entity view is the animating spirit behind the yearly studies that highlight companies that report positive earnings for accounting purposes but no current U.S. tax expense.[8] There is also suggestive experimental and statistical evidence from a variety of sources that individuals, including politicians, do hold the entity view. For example, one experiment shows that individuals will cease favoring investment incentives for corporations if it reduces their tax liability to zero.[9] Other work shows that perceptions of corporate tax avoidance do not appear to be linked to individual tax avoidance.[10] And in the early 1980s, when it became possible for corporations that could not use investment credits and other tax breaks to effectively sell them to other corporations that could use them, the politicians were most outraged by the purchasers of the tax breaks who used them to reduce their taxes, not the sellers who were the principal beneficiaries of the program.[11]

The entity view is consistent with one widely used corporate tax system. The U.S. states tax corporations by apportioning their domestic U.S. business income based on the sales in the state relative to total sales, although they sometimes use payroll and property as other factors to apportion the income. For purposes of apportioning business income, states do not ask where the corporation is incorporated or where they are headquartered.[12] They simply view the business income of all the corporate entities that operate in the state as potentially subject to tax; states are only limited by U.S. constitutional restraints on apportionment.

States sometimes give a benefit rationale for these taxes, claiming that they have the right to tax a corporation that exploits its market. But all observers know the benefits received by the corporation from operating within in a state are only very loosely connected to the taxes that are paid. A more straightforward rationale is: (1) total U.S. domestic corporate profits exist, and (2) if they are reasonably connected to a state, these profits can be subject to tax, regardless of where the corporation is headquartered or incorporated. This rationale seems to work well; no one really questions the rights of states if they fairly apportion the domestic business income of corporations. The entity view is consistent with this rationale—domestic corporate profits are a legitimate base for taxation, with no real questions raised about the ultimate owners of the corporations.

The Oxford International Tax Group advanced another alternative rationale for corporate taxation.[13] They rejected all the traditional rationales for the corporate tax but proposed a new one. They asked: suppose we could design an international tax system for taxing corporate profit—a legitimate object of taxation—that is economically efficient, robust to avoidance, relatively easier to administer than its competitors and provided an incentive for countries to adopt the proposed system? If a system met these criteria, they suggest it would be desirable. In other words, look to a system's operation and consequences, not to an underlying rationale. The authors designed two systems that they believed met all these criteria and thus were normatively desirable. Although the authors wished to eschew any deeper justifications for their tax proposals, one can certainly see the outline of the entity view of taxation in their work, which takes as a starting point that the corporate profits of worldwide multinational corporations are potentially available for taxation by countries.

Recent Trends: Crisis or Stability?

While there may be controversy over their interpretation, the two most basic facts about the trends in world corporate taxation are not really in dispute. Corporate tax revenues have been relatively stable, while corporate tax rates have declined.

With respect to corporate tax revenues, from 1990 to 2017, corporate tax revenue as a share of GDP has been either roughly stable or increasing, with the increases occurring in the less-developed countries.[14] In 2017, prior to the pandemic, average corporate tax revenue as a share of GDP averaged about 2.5 percent. In terms of the share of total tax revenues, the less-developed countries rely more heavily on the corporate tax as a source of revenue and have seen this share increase in recent years. In contrast, there is no long-run secular trend for high-income countries in their share of corporate taxes as a percent of total taxes, although from the late 1990s to 2009, the share had increased. Overall, with respect to revenues, the corporate tax picture has looked reasonably stable over the last thirty years.

In contrast to revenues, statutory tax rates (the headline rates enshrined in legislation) have fallen substantially over time.[15] Tax rates have fallen consistently over time in high-, medium- and low-income countries, from nearly 40 percent in 1990 to 25 percent by 2017. Through 2017, the United States had a 35 percent corporate rate but reduced it to 21 percent beginning in 2018, following the global trend of declining rates.

How should we interpret the different patterns for statutory tax rates and revenues? It appears to be a bit of a puzzle, which can give rise to different interpretations. Governments of the OECD countries have focused on the falling statutory rates and have decried that tax competition between countries is bringing them down over time. Implicitly, they believe that if the rates had been maintained at prior levels, then revenues from corporate taxation would be substantially higher and benefit their country's finances. Many economists do share this view that tax competition leading to lower statutory rates is a sign that the current system is unstable.[16]

An alternative perspective would emphasize the remarkable stability of corporation tax revenue as a share of GDP, particularly considering falling statutory rates. As economist Mihir Desai has observed, if we had been told thirty years ago that we would maintain the share of corporate tax revenue to GDP while cutting tax rates, we would have thought this would be an outstanding success. After all, lower tax rates reduce the total excess burden and economic distortions. To maintain revenue levels in the face of falling rates would be a real achievement.[17]

With falling statutory rates, some other factors must be providing this relative stability in revenue. There are several possible candidates. These could include an increasing share of corporate profits as a share of GDP; changes in the efficiency of collecting the corporate tax, perhaps through increased use of computer technology or other administrative innovations; or changes in the tax laws themselves that prevent the decreases in statutory rates from leading to lower effective tax rates, such as reforms to increase the corporate tax base or increased vigilance in eliminating tax sheltering activity.

Perhaps there is a political economy story that can reconcile these two perspectives on revenues and rates. Politicians and government officials have preferences over how much revenue they wish to raise from various sources. Taxes differ in many important dimensions. Some taxes may be more progressive, and some meet more political resistance than others, while others may be more conducive to economic growth. Politicians must make these challenging tradeoffs in determining their portfolio of taxes. Moreover, economic growth is often paramount. Business lobbyists have made politicians well aware of studies from economists, including those associated with the OECD, that find that corporate taxation is more detrimental to economic growth than other types of taxes.[18] If politicians find that underlying changes in the economy or in tax collection technologies would increase the share of corporate taxes in total revenue at current statutory tax rates, they will recognize the possibility of reducing statutory rates while preserving their desired share of corporate taxation. But without the change in the potential collectible corporate tax base, statutory rates would not decline.

Another way of exploring trends in corporate taxation is to calculate effective tax rates for individual firms using accounting data. Scott Dyreng and Michelle Hanlon provide a recent overview of this body of research as well as original findings.[19] They provide consistent measures of cash income taxes paid divided by pre-tax accounting or book income for both U.S. domestic corporations and U.S. multinationals. They call this measure the effective tax rate. Cash income taxes refer to actual income taxes paid in the current year to United States and foreign national governments as well as to the U.S. states.

Accounting or book income differs from taxable income in many ways, but especially with respect to timing. For example, for accounting purposes, depreciation deductions are spread over extended periods of time but are typically taken faster (accelerated) for tax purposes. Thus, looking at averages of effective tax rates over long time periods reduces these timing issues and the differences between taxable income and accounting income.

Averaging over twenty-year periods, Dyreng and Hanlon find that effective tax rates for multinational and purely domestic corporations were virtually identical at 35 percent.[20] During their period of measurement, the U.S. statutory rate was also 35 percent; however, the cash tax rate calculation applies not just to federal taxes but also to foreign and state taxes as well. Corporations paid considerable taxes to governments over this period.

From their extended analysis, the authors draw several major conclusions. First, they find considerable variability across firms in effective rates. Some firms have much higher effective tax rates than others. This variability is more pronounced over shorter time periods because of fluctuations in accounting income and tax payments. Second, there has been a recent decline in effective tax rates, but that applies equally to purely domestic as well as to multinational firms. They found this latter result puzzling as it is generally believed that multinational corporations have more potential opportunities to reduce taxes—recall the Double-Dutch Sandwich—and this has also been the focus of the activities of the OECD. Finally, firms consider complex economic, legal and political factors as they develop their tax strategies.

Transfer Pricing and the State of the International Tax System

One of the more challenging problems in today's international tax system derives from the way the major countries view the structure of multinational corporations. Although a company like Amazon sounds to the average person like a single company, it consists of myriad separately incorporated companies, partnerships and other ventures both in the United States and abroad. The international tax system generally respects the individual legal status of these separate companies. For example, if a U.S. corporation (USCorp) forms a subsidiary under local law in Ireland (IrishCorp), then the United States and other countries will treat IrishCorp as a separate company from USCorp. It will have its own filing obligations in the countries in which it operates and its own set of financial accounts reflecting the transactions it makes with its suppliers, customers and other companies.

If Ireland has a lower tax rate than the United States, then it would be possible for the two parties to engineer transactions to reduce their total taxes. Suppose IrishCorp bought aluminum rods on the world market and turned around and sold them at cost to USCorp at prevailing prices. No problem here, as USCorp is simply purchasing an input to production at normal market prices. It will have legitimate deductible expenses and IrishCorp will not generate any profits from the transaction. But now suppose that IrishCorp sold the aluminum rods for a substantially higher price, far above market prices. Then USCorp would have additional deductible expenses which would lower its taxable income in the United States and IrishCorp would have an equivalent amount of additional income in Ireland. If the tax rate in Ireland is lower than the U.S. tax rate, the tax savings from the deductions in the United States will more than offset the additional taxes on income in Ireland. Through this transaction, the two parties have reduced the total taxes they pay.

To deal with this potential problem, the United States and other countries have developed a body of law and regulations known as transfer pricing to manage transactions between related companies. The basic idea behind transfer pricing is that transactions between related parties should be evaluated as if they were on an arm's length basis—that is, as if unrelated companies conducted the transactions. Under this framework, tax authorities require that companies must ensure that their transactions with related companies should have similar terms to the hypothetical transactions that would occur if the companies were unrelated to one another. The arm's length standard is one of the key building blocks for the current system of international taxation.

Sometimes the arm's length principle is relatively easy to apply and police. If USCorp purchases standardized aluminum rods from IrishCorp, there are probably a range of transactions between unrelated parties in the open market that the companies can use to benchmark the transaction and there will be little scope for manipulating the terms of the sale to reduce taxes. But other times, this standard is much more complex to apply. There are both profound economic and legal difficulties with trying to implement the arm's length approach in practice.

From the economic point of view, there are two issues—one quite straightforward and the other more complex. The straightforward issue is that it is sometimes extremely difficult to identify comparable transactions that would occur in the market. Transfers of intellectual property often fall into this category. Depending on the nature of the property transferred and the accompanying restrictions and potential benefits, it may be difficult to decide on a comparable royalty rate for the transfer.

The deeper issue is that arm's length transactions are themselves fictions that are not necessarily meaningful for transactions within a multinational corporation or between affiliated companies. As economists have long recognized since the work of Nobel-prize winner Ronald Coase, one of the primary reasons for conducting transactions within a corporation, rather than through a market, is to provide either cost savings or synergies that will increase profits.[21] That is also one of the primary rationales for why large businesses organize themselves through a complicated web of closely held corporations.

But this insight raises immediate difficulties with any attempt to divide the income of the total business among its constituent corporations. If there are important synergies—so that the profits from operating as a single unit exceeds the profits that would result if each corporation operated independently—then there is no principled way to divide up the extra profit between the corporate entities. The whole really is greater than the sum of its parts. The arm's length method as originally applied—searching for transactions between corporations that are not part of a common group and do not possess these synergies—misconstrues the fundamental economics of modern multinational businesses. Inevitably, the economics of transfer pricing has evolved in practice to rely on other methods to better reflect the realities of modern business. But there still is no magic bullet here—the underlying economics suggest that some of the additional value created cannot neatly be assigned to any one organization.

Aside from these economic issues, there are also difficulties on the legal front. From the legal point of view, Section 482 of the U.S. Internal Revenue Code grants the Secretary of the Treasury explicit authority to address glaring problems in transfer pricing. The first sentence of Section 482 reads as follows:

> In the case of two or more organizations, trades, or businesses ... owned or controlled directly or indirectly by the same interests, the Secretary may distribute, apportion, or allocate gross income, deductions, credits, or allowances between or among such organizations, trades, or businesses, if he determines that such distribution, apportionment, or allocation is necessary in order to prevent evasion of taxes or clearly to reflect the income of any of such organizations, trades, or businesses.[22]

This code provision grants permission to the Internal Revenue Service (IRS) to adjust tax returns to prevent tax evasion or to reflect the income of the parties more accurately. Similar language first appeared in the U.S. tax code in 1928.

How would the IRS make these adjustments? The answer, codified in Treasury regulations, was the arm's length standard. Treasury regulations state explicitly that "the standard to be applied in every case is that of a taxpayer dealing at arm's length with an uncontrolled taxpayer."[23] The arm's length principle is also contained in the vast web of bilateral tax treaties between countries throughout the world and is embodied in common law in the United States through a series of court cases.

As we noted, sometimes it is difficult to find an appropriate arm's length comparison, particularly when there are transfers of intellectual property, such as patents or corporate knowledge. To attempt to deal with this issue, the 1986 Tax Reform Act added a second sentence to Section 482: "In the case of any transfer (or license) of intangible property ... the income with respect to such transfer or license shall be commensurate with the income attributable to the intangible." What this means is that in principle the IRS could look to the income that would be generated by the transfer of intangible property in making any adjustments to taxpayer returns, and not just search for comparable market transactions.

While these provisions grant broad authority to the government, the courts have struggled in applying the regulations in the tax code. It has been difficult for the courts to reconcile the traditional reliance by the government on the arm's length principle, which sought out comparable transactions in the market, with the "commensurate with income" standard that looked at the broader results of economic transactions on generating economic income, rather than on specific comparisons to market transactions.

These tensions within both the economic and legal frameworks for transfer pricing may seem very hypothetical, but they can be brought to life in a recent real-world example. In 2005 and 2006, Amazon decided to restructure its operations in Europe.[24] At that time, it had European branches in France, Germany and the United Kingdom that were still technically part of Amazon US. It decided, for legitimate business reasons, to form a separate European company to manage its European affairs. It located this company in Luxembourg which also provided a favorable tax environment, although this is incidental to our story here. The French, German and U.K. branches contributed their intangible assets—such as website technology, trademarks and customer lists—to the new Luxembourg company and, under U.S. tax law, the new European company had to pay Amazon US for the value of these intangibles. These payments would be taxable income to Amazon US. When they filed their taxes, Amazon claimed that the required payments were $225 million, which they duly included as part of their U.S. taxable income on their return. The IRS disagreed sharply with the amount. They claimed that the payments should be $3.6 billion: fourteen times larger.

Amazon made its calculation based on the separate value of the intangible assets that were transferred for the technology, trademarks and customer lists. The IRS claimed that this was a misleading way of viewing the transaction. Rather, the true value of the intangibles that were transferred were for all the knowledge from the French, German and U.K. branches taken as a whole. This could best be measured by the value of future profits of the new Luxembourg entity minus any tangible or physical assets that would be valued separately. The IRS claimed that intangibles included more than just the technology, trademarks and customer lists but also the value of the trained work force and potential growth opportunities, which were all related to the synergies between all the intangibles. This was best measured by looking at the future income that would be generated by the Luxembourg operation. This method of valuing intangible property is routinely used today.

Amazon won this fight in the U.S. Tax Court, and then prevailed again in the U.S. Ninth Circuit Court of Appeals in 2019. The Appeals Court ruled that the Treasury Regulations in effect during the time the intangibles were transferred in the restructuring required the IRS to value the intangibles on a separate basis and not look to the overall value for the transfer of knowledge. While this was a major loss for the U.S. Treasury, there was one bright spot. In its opinion, the Court recognized that the Treasury had promulgated new regulations in 2009 and Congress in 2017 added new language about intangibles to the tax statutes (a third sentence added to Section 482). In the first footnote in the opinion, the Ninth Circuit Court stated: "If this case were governed by the 2009 regulations or by the 2017 statutory amendment, there is no doubt the Commissioner's position would be correct."[25] In other words, under the new law and regulations, the IRS would have prevailed against Amazon.

Until quite recently, the IRS had a poor record in court against major corporations in their transfer price disputes. Perhaps they were hindered by the legal tightrope of trying to reconcile their evolving positions on arm's length pricing, from traditional reliance on a search for comparable transactions to relying on more general methods designed to produce economic results commensurate with income. Delays in promulgating new tax regulations to better fit the emerging intellectual property-based economy may also have been a factor.

In the last several years, however, the IRS has begun to prevail in important cases. As one of the several examples, after an initial defeat in the U.S. Tax Court, the IRS ultimately prevailed in a dispute with the Altera Corporation. In that case, the Ninth Circuit Appeals Court relied explicitly on the commensurate-with-income standard, rejecting arguments requiring literal interpretations of comparable transactions between unrelated parties for arm's length pricing.[26]

In addition to more favorable court verdicts in large transfer pricing cases, there are several other factors that will help to undergird the traditional international tax regime. First, tax rates are lower throughout the world. Lower rates limit the benefits of using aggressive transfer pricing strategies to shift profits and reduce the incentives for countries to rely on low tax rates or concessions to entice the relocation of economic activity. Second, the initial BEPS project, with its focus on tax mismatches, closed several glaring loopholes that corporations had frequently utilized.

Third, as an outgrowth of the original BEPS project, the OECD countries agreed to require large multinational firms to provide extensive data for each country in which they operate as well as for stateless income. This data encompass taxes paid and accrued, revenues from related and unrelated parties, income before taxes, equity, assets, employees and other information. This country-by-country reporting information is automatically shared with the tax authorities in other countries party to the agreement. Moreover, within the European Union, some of this information is scheduled to become public. Because of country-by-country reporting, the multinational corporations and their transfer price advisors now know that tax authorities will carefully look at the relation of reported profits and economic activity for anomalies. Large profits associated with minimal capital, or few employees will inevitably raise red flags. Profits that appear to be shifted to locales with low-tax rates and compliant tax authorities will be particularly suspect. Naturally, this will have a deterring effect on some aggressive tax planning.

Finally, minimum taxes will become more common in the next several years, with the U.S. GILTI regime in place and the European Union, in late 2022, agreeing that its member countries would enact the provisions of Pillar 2. Other major countries are likely to follow. In a regime of minimum taxes, high profits reported in low-tax jurisdictions will be subject to additional taxes in either the home country of the parent corporation or other locales. This will deter profit shifting to low-tax jurisdictions.

Taken together, the tax environment for multinational corporations will be significantly more scrutinized and more constrained going forward. But are these positive recent developments sufficient for the United States and world to continue operating with our long-standing framework for international taxation? Or are more far-reaching methods required?

Do We Need More Radical Measures?

Of the OECD two initiatives, Pillar 2 is the least radical in concept. It emulated the U.S. GILTI regime and encouraged the parent countries of multinationals to impose minimum taxes of at least 15 percent on foreign earnings on a country-by-country basis, with allowance for reasonable earnings attributable to real investments and employment. The key idea is that when most of major headquarters countries of multinationals adopt a minimum tax, it will eliminate many of the benefits of shifting profits or real activity to tax havens thereby preventing further tax competition on statutory rates.

But even this seemingly straightforward provision has been challenging to design and applies only to the largest firms. As the Pillar 2 discussion evolved, it became considerably more complex. The new regime required the OECD to develop novel accounting measures so all parties could determine whether taxes met the minimum standards. They also developed other rules to effectively force countries that had not enacted Pillar 2 provisions to impose the required top-up taxes or let other countries impose the minimum taxes.[27] The United States would also have to change GILTI to follow Pillar 2, as GILTI is not imposed on a country-by-country basis. One final question surrounding Pillar 2 is whether the cartel-like agreement among countries will survive or, as with the fate of other cartels, be chipped away over time as countries find clever ways to evade the agreement.

Pillar 1 is even more radical in conception. As originally designed, it only applies to approximately 100 extremely large and profitable nonfinancial multinationals, roughly half of which are based in the United States. For those companies, 25 percent of their excess profits (defined as exceeding 10 percent of sales) will be apportioned to countries based on their share of sales and subject to tax in their countries. Since the current group to which this applies includes the major digital companies, it can be seen as a partial substitute for the digital taxes it was designed to replace.

In the current framework, the parent country of the multinationals from whom profits are reallocated must take actions to avoid double-taxation of their headquartered multinationals. They must either provide a tax credit for taxes levied on reallocated income in other countries or exempt the reallocated income from its own taxation. Ideally, Google and Facebook would not see an overall change in their global corporate tax payments. They would avoid the digital taxes that would no longer be imposed by other countries. The U.S. Treasury would lose revenue when it provides foreign tax credits to Google or Facebook, but presumably would gain revenue from non-U.S. multinationals that would be allocating profits to the U.S. based on sales into the United States.

As it now stands Pillar 1 only applies to a limited number of firms—the largest and most profitable in the world. Given its restricted applicability and the sophistication of the firms, such a system can probably be administered through an OECD-sponsored body, though this will require complex agreements on accounting conventions and rules for measuring sales allocations to countries.

However, a larger issue is that the Pillar 1 agreement contains many arbitrary elements, which raises questions of whether it is stable in its current incarnation. A few obvious questions emerge. Why allocate only excess profits as opposed to all profits? Why should the fraction of reallocated excess profits be limited to 25 percent? Finally, why restrict the scope of Pillar 1 to only large and profitable firms? Why should not a single tax system apply equally to all firms?

It is challenging to find a principled answer to these questions. By only reallocating a fraction of excess profits, Pillar 1 still retains the basic transfer pricing system to divide up the remainder of the profits of multinational corporations.[28] An apportionment scheme is just appended to a transfer price framework. While others, including the Oxford Group, have offered similar proposals combining transfer pricing and apportionment methods, one may question whether a firm line can be drawn separating the components of total profits subject to each method.[29]

Politics will play a significant role here. Many developing countries will have a keen interest in expanding the scope of apportionment—in terms of the number of firms and the fraction of profits included—as they believe they are shortchanged and outgunned with the current, complex transfer price system. It will be hard to maintain the current limits on profit reallocation and the limited number of firms subject to Pillar 1. In the limit, the logical extension of the Pillar 1 approach would be to apportion all the profits of all multinational corporations by sales.

Assuming there are pressures to expand apportionment, it is not clear how an extension of Pillar 1 could be administered. There is no realistic prospect for a world bureaucracy that could serve as the repository for all audited financial statements of multinational corporations and the arbiter of sales allocations for all the firms doing international business throughout the world. It is difficult to see how a centralized apportionment scheme would be feasible in today's world. Are there decentralized models?

The U.S. states provide a model for a decentralized apportionment scheme. To simplify greatly, the U.S. states that tax the income of corporations start with a base of U.S. domestic corporate income and then use various indicators of local presence or factors (now predominantly sales) to apportion the income of the corporations to their respective states.[30] There is no centralized apportionment apparatus for the states—it is all decentralized. Each state enacts its own legislation that determines which firms are subject to apportionment (nexus), what is the precise tax base to be apportioned (individual firms or groups of related firms), and what factors will be used to apportion income. The states have considerable freedom in these choices, subject only to some U.S. constitutional restraints. As a result, there are major differences in the practices among the states. For example, roughly half the states use the unitary method of taxation where related firms in the same line of business are combined and subject to apportionment taken as a group. The other states apportion on an individual company-by-company basis. In terms of apportionment factors, states used to use a mixture of payroll, property and sales to apportion income, but currently most emphasize sales that are directed into the state.

No states give tax credits for corporate taxes paid to other states. The idea is that income apportioned to a state belongs to that state. Apportionment defines the source of the income. What other states do with the income they apportion to themselves is up to them. Of course, if states use different apportionment formulas (or different tax bases), there will inevitably be either double-taxation or income that is taxed nowhere. There are also special rules for the so-called nonbusiness income (typically investment income not directly connected to business operations) which is typically allocated to the place of commercial domicile for the corporation. The overall system does work, but it is messy and untidy.

The system in the U.S. states grew and evolved organically over an extended period. Both competition among the states and economic development considerations dominated changes to the state tax structures. For example, states began to realize that using sales as the primary factor to allocate profits would increase taxation of out-of-state firms and provide protection for their domestic firms.

Could such a system work internationally? There are two strong impediments to creating a decentralized international apportionment system. First, the lack of uniformity would be immense. It is hard to see what rules there would be, for example, on limiting a country's authority to tax. Would any physical presence be required, or would some threshold level of sales be sufficient? Would countries apportion corporate profits on a unitary basis or a company-by-company basis, or agree on uniform apportionment methods?

Lack of uniformity would be a major issue. No one would really want to re-create the current decentralized state system from scratch, with all its idiosyncratic features. Since national corporate tax rates are considerably higher than U.S. state tax rates, would there need to be some international body to decide disputes between countries on apportionment? At the minimum, there would need to be years of convening by the OECD or other groups to try to provide guidance to countries. All these difficulties seem overwhelming for a comprehensive system that covers all global international firms in all countries.

A second reason for questioning an international apportionment system is that it relies on an unrealistic psychological foundation about the ownership of the tax base. The system must start from the presumption that the profits of all multinational corporations are potentially subject to tax by any country. This idea of a common base seems to work in the U.S. states, where the identity and location of places of incorporation and commercial domiciles of firms do not really matter. The fact that headquarters of Amazon, Facebook and Tesla are, respectively, in the states of Washington, California and Texas is not meaningful to most U.S. residents. They are just U.S. companies, and their profits belong to U.S. residents. Under the entity view, their profits are legitimate objects of taxation, because they arise in separate legal distinct entities.

But on an international level, it is not clear that such homogenization in the tax base would be persuasive. Yes, Facebook and Amazon operate worldwide, but they are still identified as U.S. firms. Huawei, Tencent and Alibaba are clearly identified as Chinese firms. Critics of the current system of international taxation often suggest that firms no longer have a coherent national identity because they operate globally and transfer knowledge and patents into far away jurisdictions. But these critics may have overreacted and moved beyond popular sentiment and intuitions on this issue. When Pillar 1 reallocates some of Facebook's profits abroad, it certainly feels like U.S. profits are being sent abroad.

Perhaps sometime in the future corporations will lose their national identities so that apportioning a worldwide base of profits would be as unexceptional as U.S. states apportioning the U.S. domestic income of multistate firms. However, the history of apportionment methods in the United States suggests this may take some time. It took decades for states to move away from apportionment based on payroll and property to focus more on sales. In the early 1960s, Congressional hearings led to the Willis Commission Report, which, with respect to apportionment methods, contended that payroll and property were more natural apportionment factors than sales, as payroll and property corresponded most closely to where income was created.[31] At least in the early 1960s, it was perceived that business was primarily done where plant, equipment and payroll were located. That connection was what justified states' rights to tax that income. Although commerce today is less connected to the location of payroll and property, there is still a "where" in our intuitions about the business operations of Amazon, Facebook and Google. It would take a long time for residents of countries to cease making these associations for their national businesses.

Presuming these difficulties make global apportionment impossible, are there any solutions to the plausible claim by countries that digital companies are really earning profits in their country but not paying appropriate taxes? There are two basic approaches that largely preserve the current transfer pricing regime. First, we can rethink the wisdom of digital taxation. Some scholars have suggested that digital taxes are principled taxes that reach the locational rents or advantages that digital firms earn by connecting to their consumers.[32] The marginal cost to Facebook from reaching an additional consumer in France is close to zero, so any profits they earn can be seen as economic rents. From this point of view, digital taxes function like severance taxes that are used to tax the rents for the extraction of natural resources. As such they have a legitimate place in an international tax system. Not all taxes that fall on corporations need to be framed as corporate income taxes.

The second approach would be for the OECD to refine the notion of permanent establishment so that significant economic presence, not only physical presence, would be required to legitimately tax foreign enterprises. A certain threshold of sales could constitute a significant economic presence. Israel, for example, has issued rules in this regard so that sales into Israel would constitute significant economic presence.[33] U.S. states now regard economic presence as a sufficient basis for taxation. Once the right to taxation is established, there still is the question of how much income could be attributed to the newly defined permanent establishment. This would need to rely on a creative application of the arm's length principle. While this approach may not necessarily be easy to develop, it would not be beyond the creativity of modern transfer pricing economists to lay out reasonable approaches. Such an approach would fit more closely with the current international tax system. It could provide a starting point for attributing income from digital sales to a country—without requiring a wholesale rewrite of the international tax system.

Concluding Thoughts

A precise rationale for taxing global corporate income is elusive from a purely theoretical point of view, but countries (and states) will not be stopped by theoretical niceties from seeking additional revenue, reaching all income and satisfying the psychological urge to tax profitable entities. The question is always how to do this in a complex, multipolar world without damaging commerce and preserving international comity

The last decade has witnessed dramatic changes in the practice of corporate and international taxation. The responses of the international community to increasingly sophisticated tax planning by multinational corporations and their willing country partners have transformed the landscape. There is a sense that the old system of taxation is no longer up to the task but it is not clear what will eventually replace it.

The old system gave primacy to the source country, the place where the operating income of a corporation was presumed to be earned. But it has become increasingly difficult to pin down the precise source of income with increasingly integrated multinational corporations and new methods of reaching consumers in the digital age. The traditional system relied on using transfer pricing methods to decide which country had the primary taxing rights. A new, embryonic system, as exemplified in the OECD Pillar 1, may potentially abandon this practice, and simply seek to divide total corporate profits for international business by formulas.

In this chapter, I suggest that the OEDC and its Inclusive Framework may have underestimated the benefits from the reforms that have already been made in the last decade in closing international loopholes and shoring up transfer pricing methods. Besides they may have also underestimated the difficulties, both in methodology and in national psychology, of a new system based on dividing global corporate business profits by formula. There also will be challenges to the emerging minimum tax regime. Historically, many countries have used the tax system to attract investment; developing countries do not want to miss their own opportunity.

International taxation is a good example where the controversies arise because of a series of underlying factors—the economics of multinational corporations, the psychology of taxation, evolving legal standards, administrative challenges and a healthy dose of international politics. Solutions in the international realm require careful attention to all these elements.

Notes

1 For a full explanation, see Kleinbard, "Stateless Income."
2 As referenced in Kleinbard, "Stateless Income," 706.
3 U.S. Senate Committee on Finance, "Tax Talk: The $2+ Trillion Lockout."
4 The OECD summarizes their work at OECD BEPS ACTIONS.
5 There are other rationales for the corporate tax, such as taxing nonprofits or foreign shareholders who would not otherwise be subject to U.S. tax without a corporate tax.
6 My discussion here was influenced by Devereux et al., *Taxing Profits in a Global Economy*, Chapter 2.
7 The United States has a set of rules that make it difficult for individuals to hold shares in foreign companies that are primarily invested in passive income. These are known as the PFIC rules—passive foreign investment companies.
8 See, for example, Institute on Taxation and Economic Policy, "55 Corporations Paid $0 in Federal Taxes on 2020 Profits."
9 Sheffrin, "Perceptions of Fairness in the Crucible of Tax Policy."
10 Sheffrin, Steven and Rujun Zhao, "Public Perceptions of the Tax Avoidance of Corporations and the Wealthy."

11 Sheffrin, "What Have We Done to the Corporate Tax System?"

12 For the so-called nonbusiness income such as dividends and royalties, the home of the corporation does matter.

13 See, Devereux et al., *Taxing Profits in a Global Economy*, Chapter 2.

14 Devereux et al., *Taxing Profits in a Global Economy*, Table 1.1b.

15 Devereux et al., *Taxing Profits in a Global Economy*, Figure 1.2.

16 The instability of the current regime is a main theme in Devereux et al., *Taxing Profits In A Global Economy*.

17 Desai, "Myths and Mysteries of the Corporate Income Tax."

18 Arnold et al., "Tax Policy for Economic Recovery and Growth." Also, see McBride, "What is the Evidence on Taxes and Growth?" For a contrary view, see Saez and Zucman, *The Triumph of Injustice*.

19 Dyreng and Hanlon, "Tax Avoidance and Multinational Firm Behavior,".

20 Ibid. Table 10-1, p. 376.

21 Coase, "The Nature of the Firm."

22 Section 482 of the Internal Revenue Code.

23 U.S. Treasury Regulations 1.482-1 (b)(1).

24 This summary draws on the U.S. 9th Circuit Opinion in 2019 in Amazon.Com & Subsidiaries v. the Commissioner of Internal Revenue.

25 Footnote 1, p. 6 in Amazon.Com and Subsidiaries v. the Commissioner of Internal Revenue.

26 Altera v Commissioner 9th Circuit, 2019.

27 The most recent version of Pillar 2 contains a provision (known as UTPR, the under-taxed profit rule) that allows for countries other than the parent country to impose additional taxes if minimums are not met.

28 Pillar 1 does contain discussions about using standard rules of thumb for marketing and distribution costs (amount B) to simplify transfer pricing.

29 The Oxford Group's Residual Profit Allocation by Income method is based on the rationale that for standard production and services transfer pricing methods are reasonable, but the remainder of profits are apportioned by sales.

30 There are complicated issues and disputes about how and when foreign operations are included in the apportioned tax base.

31 The Willis commission report was authored by the Special Subcommittee on State Taxation of Interstate Commerce and entitled "State Taxation of Interstate Commerce." For a discussion, see Drenkard, "The Willis Commission: The Most Important Tax Study You Probably Haven't Read."

32 Cui, "The Digital Services Tax: A Conceptual Defense."

33 Orbitax, "Israel Adopts Virtual PE Concept Based on a Significant Digital Presence."

Chapter 5

COMPETING PERSPECTIVES
ON TAX FAIRNESS

Controversies about taxation often revolve around different conceptions of what constitutes fairness. Sometimes the debates are very straightforward as when politicians and the press wrangle over who really benefitted from the latest tax cut. At other times, the debates become very philosophical, particularly when the topic is whether to use taxation to redistribute income. Concepts based on social solidarity confront those that focus on individual economic rights.

Broad philosophical debates are engaging and challenging and often reflect at a very abstract level broad fundamental differences of opinion in our society. But they only loosely connect with the average citizen's beliefs about what constitutes tax fairness. Popular beliefs can best be understood not through the lens of philosophy, but through the lens of social psychology. Surprisingly, the beliefs and attitudes the public holds about taxation—what I have dubbed in another setting folk justice—can explain some of the puzzling behavior we witness in our everyday politics of taxation.[1]

In this chapter, I will first briefly explore the broad philosophical debates about tax fairness, starting with the standard normative perspective offered by economists and recent extensions. This is a natural starting place to begin the discussion of overarching, theoretically oriented perspectives on tax fairness. This provides a nice introduction to the grand debates on distributive justice. I then turn to the quite different beliefs and perspectives of the public—folk justice. As we will see, the concept of fair procedure as well as desert or deservingness play a key role in public attitudes. Whether market rewards are deserved is a highly contested issue. Finally, these discussions lead to the practical issue of what types of taxation are not only consistent with conventional perspectives on progressive taxation but also consistent with concepts of desert.

Optimal Tax Theory

A convenient beginning place for exploring the theoretical dimensions of tax fairness is the economic theory of optimal taxation. Within economics, this is the basis for discussions of tax fairness. Optimal tax theory has distinguished roots in the history of economic thought. The polymath Frank Ramsey first explored how to raise tax revenue while minimizing the distortions or excess burdens that accompany raising of revenue through taxation (discussed in Chapter 2). Ramsey's focus was on taxes placed on individual commodities, such as sales or excise taxes.

But the modern incarnation of optimal tax theory began with the work of James Mirrlees in 1971 on optimal income taxation.[2] He developed a complex, but rigorous method to trade off social goals of redistribution with the loss of economic efficiency that taxation inevitably entails. The reach of this work has been profound; philosophers of social justice routinely reference it, and within economics, some scholars have used it to recast the entire field of public economics.[3]

Mirrlees casts his model in a utilitarian framework, where outcomes are ultimately assessed on how individuals perceive their own satisfaction. Individual well-being or utility depends positively on consumption and negatively on the amount of work individuals choose to perform. Utility is comparable across individuals. In addition, the additional benefits of higher consumption decrease as income increases; that is, there is diminishing marginal utility of consumption. The government has a social welfare function that judges or ranks social outcomes based on the individual utilities. As one example, the government might simply add up the total utilities for all individuals and choose outcomes that maximize that sum. That formulation would be classic utilitarianism. The social welfare function could be more or less redistributive, but in all cases reflects a social judgment that must be made. If individuals have identical utility functions, then diminishing marginal utility implies that taking a dollar from a rich person and giving it to a poor person would raise total utility—the loss in utility from the rich person would be outweighed by the gain of utility from the poorer person. If our goal was to simply allocate a fixed pot of income, then equalizing income would maximize total social utility.

But the total level of income is not a fixed pot, it depends on how much individuals work. Here is where Mirrlees's contribution comes in. He made the realistic assumption that individuals differed in their skill levels, but the government could not directly observe those skill levels, only the total income individuals earn. Taxes must be based on income, not skill levels. Income taxes, however, will discourage work effort and reduce the amount available to finance public services or redistribute income. Mirrlees explicitly worked out the trade-offs between efficiency and equity within this framework. In general, less redistribution will be desired if individuals are sensitive to higher tax rates and reduce their efforts accordingly. More redistribution will be desired if utility diminishes sharply with income, or if the social welfare function exhibits a strong preference for equality. Economists applying this framework with their own auxiliary assumption come to different conclusions about how much tax progressivity would be optimal.[4]

In the last 15 years, there have been important developments that both critique and extend the optimal tax framework. Gregory Mankiw and Matthew Weinzierl provided a clever critique of the utilitarian basis of standard optimal tax theory.[5] They noted that if there were perfect information about abilities, the government could simply levy higher lump-sum or fixed levies on higher ability taxpayers without distorting their behavior because their taxes no longer depended upon their income. While we do not observe abilities directly, we do observe some variables correlated with ability. It turns out that height is correlated with wages in the market.

Mankiw and Weinzierl show how to incorporate height into an optimal tax framework and have separate tax schedules depending on the taxpayer's height. Adding height to the tax schedule allows taxes to be a function of both height and income, giving the government an opportunity to fine-tune its social welfare calculations and permit more redistribution with less distortion.

Mankiw and Weinzierl were not advocating for another line to be added to IRS Form 1040 where individuals would put in their government-determined height. They along with most people would have difficulty basing an income tax on variables such as height, race or sex. Yet all these variables are potentially available to the government and difficult to alter. Rather, Mankiw and Weinzierl were cleverly critiquing the utilitarian-based optimal tax theory and arguing that its moral foundations are suspect.

Recognizing that other ideas of fairness and justice may not be subsumed within the utilitarian model, economists have developed alternative models that incorporate some of the ethical notions we discuss later in this chapter. Weinzierl modified the optimal tax framework to allow for taxation to be tied to the perceived benefits of public goods, which, in turn, are related to the individual's income earning potential. He also explored other normative objectives, such as requiring an equal sacrifice from individuals from the free market outcome.[6]

Emmanuel Saez and Stefanie Stantcheva develop a flexible framework to assess small changes in taxes using weights on observed earning levels that can incorporate nonutilitarian considerations, such as libertarian values, equality of opportunity or the elimination of poverty.[7] However, Itai Sher demonstrates that this approach may not deliver consistent global judgments of social welfare; that is, social welfare judgments in the Saez and Stantcheva framework may not be transitive and cycle (A is preferred to B, B is preferred to C, but C is preferred to A).[8] In other work, Mark Fleurbaey and Francois Maniquet provide a comprehensive review of the challenges of incorporating nonutilitarian considerations into public finance models.[9] They suggest that individual utility indices can be flexibly varied to capture different ethical notions of fairness and then incorporated into social welfare functions.

Let us take a step back. This more recent work on optimal taxation is designed to take alternative ethical notions and incorporate them into economic models that incorporate individual responses to taxation. The output of these models is a set of tax and transfer rates that combine economic efficiency and the ethical notions. Different ethical premises will generate different tax rate schedules. It is also possible to reverse engineer this process: what ethical notions correspond to existing tax and transfer rate schedules?[10] Of course, it may stretch credulity to believe that existing tax schedules follow from applications of optimal tax theory. Regardless, the basis of all this recent work are alternative ethical world views, to which I now turn.

The Grand Debates

Optimal tax theory provides a nice transition to philosophical accounts of justice. One striking version of a social welfare function would be to maximize the utility or well-being of the least well-off in society, or a max–min social welfare function. Social outcomes would be judged only by the welfare of the worst-off in society. Inequalities in income could be tolerated but only if they improve the welfare of the least well-off. Within the optimal tax framework, this would be the social welfare function that produced the most redistribution.

We associate the max-min concept with the philosopher John Rawls in his 1971 book, *A Theory of Justice*.[11] Rawls was not a utilitarian and developed his views about social justice within a different framework. He asked us to envision what choices we would make for the range of after-tax, after-transfer economic outcomes if we were collectively behind a veil of ignorance where we would not know what our specific native abilities, endowments or even personal ambitions would be. Rawls argued that in this setting we would choose to ensure that individuals had not only basic rights and liberties but also social inequalities would only be justified if they improved the welfare of the least well-off in our society.

Rawls's book set the basis for subsequent decades of discussion of justice and social welfare and has had broad social influence.[12] For example, while not following Rawls in detail, Liam Murphy and Thomas Nagel embrace Rawls' sensibility of ensuring social justice in their philosophical book on taxation, *The Myth of Ownership*. They argue that after all taxes and transfers have taken place, the resulting distribution of income should have certain properties, particularly providing a robust social minimum for the poor.

In 1974, philosopher Robert Nozick, a Harvard colleague of Rawls, published *Anarchy, State, and Utopia* which explicitly broke from this social solidarity tradition. Famously, he characterized Rawls's views and other attempts to outline the pattern of a just society as end-state views. According to Nozick, standard theories of distributive justice are ahistorical end-state theories, specifying that the distribution of income or wealth in society should have a certain pattern, regardless of how history evolved, and the current distribution of income arose. Nozick rejected these end-state views and developed a libertarian framework that eschewed end-state principles. He developed a theory of how both just acquisition of original resources in the past and just transactions between people would produce an overall just and fair outcome. Whatever final pattern of income that arose after this historical process transpired was just if its underlying components were also just. As Nozick famously argued, if fans collectively want to pay great sums to see Wilt Chamberlin (a famous 7' 1" basketball star from the 1960s and 1970s) demolish his opponents on the court, thereby earning Chamberlin a great fortune, that is a just outcome, even if the willing choices of fans generate great social inequality.

Nozick's work spurred a large literature emphasizing rights-based theories of economic justice. Rights-based theories of justice tend to be much more deferential to actual social outcomes and suspicious of great redistributions in the name of end-state fairness. Supporters of this view would typically prefer limited government with low-tax burdens. In the United States, economic rights have often taken a back-seat to other rights considered more fundamental by constitutional scholars, such as free speech or freedom of religion. The libertarian philosopher Eric Mack notes that without much argument some philosophers place freedom of speech and religion "as markedly more crucial to human autonomy than the grubby freedom to operate a food truck despite the city council machinations of restaurant owners."[13] Mack and other libertarians emphasize that economic freedom should also be seen as essential to human freedom and flourishing. As we discuss below, the psychological concept of equity theory and the philosophical notion of desert reinforce this libertarian approach to economic outcomes.

Not all libertarian-based theories rely on the Nozickian natural rights principles. As Mack discusses extensively, another strong justification for enforcing property rights and claims to ownership stems from a tradition developed by David Hume and Frederick Hayek which highlights the social efficiency of norms that sustain property rights.[14] For example, Hume emphasized that the stability of ownership rights eases social tensions and helps to promote effective social interactions.

Most individuals have both Rawlsian and Nozickian intuitions. We do care about the welfare of the poor but often regale at the fortunes of pop stars and athletes. Social psychologists have looked more carefully at public attitudes toward fairness and have developed some provocative generalizations about popular perceptions of fairness in economic settings.

Folk Justice and Taxation

What does the public believe in tax fairness? In contrast to end-state theorists who focus primarily on distribution, individuals are often much more concerned about process and procedure than they are in purely distributional issues or "who gets what." Social psychologists describe this as procedural justice. In addition, individuals are also sensitive to the role of individual effort and initiative in determining economic rewards. The focus on the connection between effort and rewards is known as equity theory, which leads to an idea that individuals "deserve" what they earn.[15]

Procedural justice

In ordinary life, we often associate fairness with outcomes, who gains and who loses. We are not alone in this sentiment. The broad philosophical tradition of utilitarianism, which provides the foundations for most research in economics and taxation, starts from this position judging desirable states based on outcomes.

But a large established body of research, cutting across social psychology, legal scholarship and research in compliance with the law all suggest that overall social satisfaction is not just based on outcomes but also on the process or procedures through which the outcomes are derived. The literature on procedural justice or procedural fairness is now over forty-five years old. It originated in the study of the role of procedures in the legal system, then expanded into broader social settings including law enforcement and policing, labor relations and acceptance or acquiescence of citizens to political outcomes.

Many aspects of procedure have been found to be important in differing contexts, but two features stand out in a wide range of studies. The first is voice or the ability to engage and participate in the process generating outcomes and to tell one's story. The second is respectful and dignified treatment in social interactions.

Tom Tyler and Alan Lind have emphasized the logic behind the desire for respectable treatment.[16] Individuals make gains through social cooperation, but social cooperation requires that we cede control to others. However, placing ourselves at the mercy of others also exposes us to maltreatment and a variety of dangers, spanning mental, emotional or even physical dangers. Fair and open decision-making processes reduce these risks and allow us to enjoy the benefits of social cooperation with less individual exposure. To the extent that these instincts become ingrained in our nature through a process of social evolution, we may embrace fair processes for other reasons than immediate monetary payoffs.

Procedural justice has great explanatory power for understanding tax revolts and tax compliance. As we highlighted in Chapter 1, the miners in Kalgoorlie, Australia, staged a massive protest against the Australian Tax Office because they felt they were being treated arbitrarily and singled out for the use of what they believed to be legitimate tax shelters for their newfound earnings.

In the United States, the Internal Revenue Service (IRS) in the late 1990s was also forced to change its tone with taxpayers and build in more respectful treatment after a series of Congressional hearings focusing on potential abuses. Today, the agency tries not only to balance both a legitimate enforcement effort against noncompliance but also to provide some semblance of customer service.

Procedural justice concerns also directly affect the imposition and administration of taxes. Part of the reason that the property tax in the United States has often been unpopular can be attributed to the lack of voice of property owners.[17] Property tax assessments often appear arbitrary—and even if a homeowner recognized that their property has appreciated, they may feel that they are treated differentially from their neighbors or from businesses. This certainly was the case with the most major property tax revolt in the United States in recent years, Proposition 13 in California. Seemingly out of nowhere, homeowners received new tax bills with massive tax increases. The result was a voter revolt and the institution of a completely new property tax system, with taxpayer protections built in. Most states now have a series of built-in tax limitation protections to prevent the imposition of sudden increases in property taxes.

Voice is also important in property taxation. Successful property tax reforms have relied on extensive consultation and opportunities for participation. For example, Wales was successful in implementing a major property revaluation after several years of careful consultation with the public, but England, operating under the same general system, was not.[18]

Providing fair procedures for taxpayers and opportunities for voice is an ongoing challenge for tax agencies who must operate extremely complex tax systems with many competing demands. Small businesses often feel caught in the middle. They experience high compliance burdens from a complex tax code typically designed for larger entities and are forced to rely on expensive private tax advisors to navigate the system. As we discussed in Chapter 4, the system for taxing foreign income has become increasingly complex and small businesses expanding abroad now face significantly more complex tax environments.

Another aggrieved group with little opportunities for voice are U.S. citizens and green card holders living permanently abroad who must file U.S. taxes and are subject to extensive regulations. This group includes the so-called accidental Americans who live abroad and identify as residents of foreign countries but may have U.S. citizenship from their parents or their early childhood. For example, in 2016, the U.K.'s Boris Johnson, who was born in the United States and lived there until he was five years old, renounced his citizenship after a prolonged battle with the IRS over owing capital gains taxes on an apartment he sold in North London.[19] Moreover, with the passage in 2010 of the Foreign Account Taxpayer Compliance Act (FATCA), foreign financial institutions must report holdings of any U.S. citizen or green card holder to the United States. This has made it difficult for many U.S. taxpayers living abroad to navigate banking and other financial activities as foreign financial institutions face increased compliance burdens with the accounts from U.S. taxpayers.

Equity theory

Another important component of public attitudes toward taxation is based on equity theory, which we introduced in Chapter 1. As we briefly highlighted, equity theory is a school in psychology based on well-documented evidence that individuals feel the most satisfied when the rewards or returns they receive from their actions are related to the input or efforts they have made. Outputs need to be commensurate with inputs. Individuals are dissatisfied both if their rewards fall short of their efforts or their rewards outstrip their efforts. More broadly, equity theory suggests that societal institutions should be structured to provide rewards based on individual contributions and effort.

With respect to economic activity, the strongest psychological implication of equity theory is that individuals will have a strong mental connection to their earnings. It also implies that, barring unusual circumstances, there should be a strong connection between work effort and the receipt of funds. In the United States, there are strong feelings about requiring work to receive payments from the state—this feeling is related to equity theory. Welfare-oriented programs require work effort, especially for single individuals capable of entering the labor force. Even Social Security payments are based on past work experience.

With respect to the tax system, equity theory weighs in on the side of a meaningful role for before-tax income, contrary to the arguments of Liam Murphy and Thomas Nagel who focus on after-tax income.[20] Although individuals may recognize that they owe taxes for necessary social obligations, they feel attached to their before-tax earnings. These earnings are signifiers of their effort and even perhaps their true worth as individuals. That is why seeing taxes being taken out of paychecks is often a painful experience—even if the taxes are perceived as fair, they somehow sever the relationship between individual effort and rewards.

Desert theory

Equity theory in psychology bears a close resemblance to the philosophical theory of desert. The theory has a simple structure: an individual (I) deserves an outcome (P) based on some criterion (W). In the economic context, the outcome (P) would be a monetary payment and the basis (W) would be some measure of work or effort. But this definition immediately raises the question of whether individuals deserve what they earn in a market economy. If so, the grounds for income redistribution become weaker than if they did not deserve their earnings.

Philosophers distinguish between two types of deserts. The first and least controversial type of desert is institutional. As an example, consider a corporate competition that establishes a process for whom will be promoted among all the contenders to become the CEO and earn a vast level of compensation. Once the rules of the game and prizes for the winners are established by the board of directors of the corporation, competition among the contenders will ensue and a winner will emerge. If the winner played cleanly by the corporate rules, he or she would clearly deserve the CEO compensation, no matter how large the compensation or whether the new CEO had any particularly admirable virtues. The winner simply prevailed under the well-established rules set by the board of directors.

A second, and more controversial type of desert, is known as preinstitutional. Here, we would argue that another new CEO, by virtue of her hard work, ingenuity and value to the company, deserved her large salary regardless of the precise rules of the corporate promotional competition. Her business acumen and moral qualities make her fully deserving of the new position.

Equity theory in psychology and its philosophical counterpart of preinstitutional desert both tie rewards to effort. They are framed without reference to institutional structures. Applying this principle to markets, they lead us away from policies of redistribution of income and toward the acceptance of whatever outcomes result from market transactions. But this line of thought has come under critical scrutiny from many philosophers.

Tax scholars are probably most familiar with the critique of preinstitutional desert from the work of Murphy and Nagel who argue that the ability of individuals to earn high market salaries depend on a set of institutions supported by taxes, including certain specific property rights. Consequently, individuals do not have a presumptively just claim or deserve their before-tax earnings, as they are dependent on an extensive system of tax-supported property rights.

John Rawls provided another well-known critique of preinstitutional desert. His argument goes beyond Murphy and Nagel by questioning whether individual motivation or effort can ever be any basis for assessing justice. Rawls asserted that socially determined differences in character, effort and motivation all create unfair advantages, which are distinct from differences in traditional property rights.

Another prominent strand of philosophical thought—luck egalitarianism—maintains with Rawls that individuals do not deserve material or natural advantages. It departs from Rawls, however, in permitting an important role for recognizing and rewarding individual effort; once we neutralize for the effects of brute luck in terms of endowments or other natural advantages, we can base rewards on desert. For luck egalitarians, desert would only have a role to play after significant redistributions of income and resources have occurred that neutralize brute luck.

On the other hand, other philosophers believe desert should play a larger role in our assessments of justice than even envisioned by luck egalitarians. David Miller recounts several scenarios of conduct which warrant desert, even though luck was clearly involved. A young scientist happens to land a job in a laboratory with a promising line of research and she fortuitously has an insight that lands her a Nobel Prize. Or a young man is walking on a levee and notices a young toddler has fallen into the river and jumps in and saves her. In both cases, we still admire the scientist for her discovery and the young man for his bravery, even though circumstances placed them in situations in which their talents could shine.[21]

Preparation to take advantage of luck is also important according to Miller. This idea is nicely illustrated in a quote attributed to the golfer Gary Player: "The harder you work, the luckier you get."[22] Implicit in this maxim is the notion that it is difficult to separate luck from preparation. If someone prepares carefully for an event or contest and succeeds in part because they were lucky, we typically will say they deserved to succeed if the preparation was sufficient.

Since philosophers differ on their view of desert, what do ordinary people think? Philosophers Christopher Freiman and Shaun Nichols explored commonly held ideas on desert through online experiments.[23] A control group was given the following statement to read: "Suppose that some people make more money than others solely because they have genetic advantages." They were then asked whether such people deserve the extra money and whether it is fair for them to receive the extra money. They labeled the control group the abstract condition, in that respondents were asked about general principles of justice.

In contrast, the experimental group was presented with concrete situations. One of the treatment groups received the following statement to read:

Suppose that Amy and Beth both want to be professional jazz singers. They both practice singing equally hard. Although jazz singing is the greatest natural talent of both Amy and Beth, Beth's vocal range and articulation is naturally better than Amy's because of differences in genetics. Solely as a result of this genetic advantage, Beth's singing is much more impressive. As a result, Beth attracts bigger audiences and hence gets more money than Amy.[24]

Respondents in this group were then asked whether Beth deserved more money and whether it was fair.

What were the results? In the abstract condition, respondents did not believe that those with genetic advantages deserved more money, nor was it fair for them to do so. In contrast, in the concrete setting respondents believed that Beth both deserved more money and that it was fair for her to receive it. One way to put this result is that in theory, people support neutralizing natural advantages, but in practice and when confronted with real-world situations, they would loathe to do so. Thus, in practical situations, people may reject the intuitions from luck egalitarianism that brute luck must be neutralized. We can see this phenomenon in the way we admire and venerate sporting figures. No one really questions whether Roger Federer, Rafael Nadal, Novak Djokovic or Serena Williams deserved their financial fortunes.

Moving away from pure philosophical discussions, we can explore the concept of desert from an economic lens. At a basic level, the market economy does reward individuals for producing products that others will want. The price of a product will reflect demand from society. With respect to wages, traditional neoclassical theory dictates that in competitive markets individuals will receive the value of the marginal product. That is, they will receive in wages what their individual contribution adds to the value of production. One can argue that this embodies a sense of fairness—people receive what they contribute. Even some academic economists share this intuition of the fairness of markets. Harvard economist Gregory Mankiw advocated abandoning utilitarian intuitions and basing tax policy on what he called just deserts.[25]

While this idea is seductive, there are major difficulties with associating market outcomes with desert. Here, I want to focus on what I consider the three most important problems linking market outcomes and deservingness. First, markets allocate commodities and labor to their highest and best use—maximizing the value of a given set of resources—given underlying demand for goods and services. Prices and wages are determined in the process as a function of supply and demand. The difficulty here is that market demands depend on the initial distribution of income or endowments and, furthermore, demands can shift for a host of reasons that are not clearly related to any notion of desert. To take one example, thirty years ago salaries for dermatologists were not much higher than those for doctors who specialized in internal medicine. Today, with changes in preferences for skin care and new technologies, the gap between the salaries of the two types of doctors has widened substantially.[26] Dermatologists in their 50s now earn relative salaries that they realistically could not have expected to earn when they made their original decisions on specialties.[27] In what sense do those dermatologists deserve their higher salaries? We certainly understand from the principles of supply and demand why they earn their higher salaries, but what moral principle corresponds to this shift in demand?

The second problem stems from deviations from the ideal of a competitive market, such as increasing returns to scale and the related superstar phenomenon. Using music as an example, Michael Jackson produced brilliant pop albums in his time and earned a massive fortune, significantly higher than many other talented musical performers. Part of the difference in salaries may have been attributable to his excellence, but certainly another reason for the vast difference between him and other performers was the technological advances that allowed his music to be distributed and consumed through new digital and video formats at virtually zero marginal cost. Ludwig Beethoven may have also shared similar market dominance in his age, but he needed to perform in person—a much less-efficient way to disseminate music. David Bowie may have deserved to earn more than other performers in the predigital past, but many would contend that the difference in compensation exceeds the differences in musical talent.

In another example, we noted that no one appears to resent that the male tennis stars of the twenty-first century earned great fortunes. But compare their fortunes to the earnings of magnificent tennis players in the twentieth century such as Rod Laver or Billy Jean King. The differences between the salaries of these stars reflect the growth of the worldwide viewing and advertising market for tennis, along with the growth of media that fueled the popularity of the sport. One cannot credibly claim that Rod Laver or Billie Jean King are less deserving than the other great tennis players.

We have already highlighted a third key issue connecting market outcomes and deservingness—the role of luck or fortune. Being in the right place at the right time or having fortuitous events can greatly influence one's market worth. From the practical economics side, it is difficult to distinguish effort from pure luck. Two individuals chose stocks to fill out a portfolio decades ago. One chose the upstart on-line bookstore Amazon, the other the now defunct bookstore Borders. We now know how that turned out for the investors. But did they really have the foresight and knowledge in advance, so they are deserving of their relative fortunes?

Do markets produce outcomes for individuals that they deserve? Both from the philosophical and economic perspective various types of luck pose important issues. As we have seen there is ongoing debate among philosophers about how luck interacts with desert. Some philosophers like Rawls believe that any type of luck, including genetic advantages, breaks the link between preinstitutional desert and market outcomes, although some experimental evidence suggests otherwise. Other philosophers such as David Miller do find certain types of luck compatible with desert. Brute luck such as winning a lottery may not be deserved but being in the right place to save a drowning infant would still warrant praise or perhaps a monetary award. Similarly, luck egalitarians do believe that option luck which arises from deliberate choices by individuals is a legitimate basis for inequalities, but inequalities arising from brute luck are not legitimate. Other commentators believe option luck produces unjust outcomes as well.[28]

Qualified perceptions of fairness

Up to now, I have discussed popular ideas based on process, procedure and individual initiative. But there is considerable evidence that basic perceptions of fairness in the division of the economic pie play a fundamental role in our deep-seated beliefs about justice. The evidence for this proposition comes from a variety of sources, but especially from the extensive results of the well-known ultimatum game in which a proposer offers a division of say $10 to a decider who can either accept the offer or reject it; in the latter case, both parties receive nothing. Countless experiments have shown that participants in the ultimatum game do _not_ play the game in the way predicted by purely rational game theory—that is the offers are not $.01 or some small amount. Typically, proposers offer between 30 and 40 percent of the total amount, with a 50-50 split often the mode. Moreover, offers less than 20 percent of the total are frequently rejected.[29]

Economists have developed elegant economic theories of fairness to incorporate the results of the ultimatum and related dictator games, which are
games where one party simply decides on a division of the resources. One
popular model is based on the idea of inequity aversion which means that
individual preferences are such that they dislike inequitable outcomes. Ernst
Fehr and Klaus Schmidt develop this theory in detail and show how it can be
used to explain a wide variety of economic phenomena, including the experimental results in game theory.[30] Other economic models focus on the intentions of the parties in social interactions. By developing models that reflect
these results, the idea is that fairness is an inherent part of social interactions
that must be understood by social scientists.

More recent research indeed suggests that the sheer simplicity and ele-
gance of the ultimatum game might be disguising some important factors
in individuals' actual assessments of fairness as they occur in ordinary life.
In daily life, incomes for most individuals are not received from an outside
experimenter but from work. Several experiments have revealed that the origin of the funds to be distributed in a dictator game matters to the outcome.
Consider the interesting study by Robert Oxoby and John Spraggon.[31] They
explored games where either the dictators or the recipients earned a level of
wealth prior to the beginning of the game by performance on a standardized
test. Dictators would only respect earned income in their allocations. They
interpreted their results as consistent with equity theory.

This brief survey of philosophical, economic and popular ideas of fairness
poses a dilemma for designing tax policy. The intuitions of the public—who
vote and elect legislators—is sympathetic to the notion of desert, but even
the public recognizes its limits and insists on some reasonable distribution
of resources, perhaps to the least well-off in society. Philosophers and economists are typically in the Rawlsian or utilitarian optimal taxation camp,
although there are important exceptions. Perhaps all parties agree that we
want to encourage entrepreneurs to be prepared to seek out opportunities for
new ideas and products and recognize that this requires appropriate rewards,
even when the opportunities partly arise by chance. Are there tax policies
that can be sensitive to all these demands?

Tax Policies Compatible with Intuitions of Desert

What if we took desert seriously as its own criteria and asked what tax policies
would be consistent with our intuitive notions of desert? For this exercise, we
simply need to believe that there is *some* element of preinstitutional desert in
our social judgments. Thinking through the implications of desert can potentially lead us in several different directions and with different implications for

progressivity of taxation. There are five different areas of taxation that can in principle be influenced by the concept of desert: rejecting utilitarian balancing, the treatment of windfalls, the distinction between earned versus unearned income, inheritance versus estate taxes and consumption versus income taxation. The last two topics require some auxiliary psychological assumptions.

Rejection of utilitarian balancing

Rejecting the utilitarian calculus of trading off one person's utility for another would place limits on the range of potential redistribution away from the rich to either the poor or the middle-class. We would not use the argument that the marginal utility of the last dollar declines as income increases to justify redistribution. The value of the last dollar Elon Musk earns may be extremely low, relative to others, but this does not serve as a basis for taxation. To the extent that Musk materially participated in the creation of innovative and marvelous products valued by the market, we would not target his earnings (just because they are large) for redistribution, even if he had been fortunate with circumstantial or option luck.

Taxing windfalls

The principle of desert suggests we should tax windfalls due to luck at higher rates. For example, winners of lotteries who had minimal active involvement in securing their earnings would not deserve their income and could be subject to a higher rate or perhaps a surcharge. Bonus payments to officials whose companies receive public bailouts might also fall into this category.

The practical difficulties of distinguishing option luck (where retaining economic returns may be consistent with desert) from brute luck (where they are not) might lead us to draw the windfall exception narrowly. Even those with faith in government generally will recognize how difficult it would be for any government agency to administer a broad program of taxing undeserved windfalls. Given all the practical difficulties in administering government programs to compensate individuals for adverse outcomes that the noted lawyer and expert Kenneth Feinberg highlights, one can imagine how difficult it would be in practice to administer programs to tax them based on deservingness.[32]

Some common notions of fairness also suggest that we may not want to tax windfalls at confiscatory rates. In the dictator game, dictators do not keep all the proceeds but do give some away to the second party. In some sense, taxing windfalls can be seen as a reverse dictator game, in that the government or society decides how much of the windfall to take.

Earned vs. unearned income

Historically, the concept of desert appears to have influenced the tax policy treatment of earned versus unearned income. At various times, our tax code in the United States and other countries have made this distinction, with income from capital—interest, dividends and capital gains—dubbed "unearned income" and taxed at higher rates. In the 1970s in the United States, for example, dividends and interest payments were taxed at a maximum rate of 70 percent compared to 50 percent for wage income or earned income. Even the supply-side U.S. Treasury Secretary Andrew Mellon once advocated for a lower tax rate on earned income. However, income from capital gains has always been treated more favorably primarily because our system typically requires a voluntary act to realize income, which is under the control of the individual. As we have discussed in Chapter 2, high capital gains rates may cause a decrease in realizations. In addition, there may be concerns about the taxation of nominal and not real capital gains on assets held for long periods of time. Neither of these reasons arise because income from capital gains is more deserving than income received in the form of dividends or interest. By 1981, the United States abandoned the distinction between earned and unearned income but does preserve the distinction between ordinary income and capital gains.

This application of desert theory runs counter to a great deal of current thinking on tax policy. As we discussed in Chapter 3, there are strong economic efficiency reasons to tax capital income at a lower rate than wages. However, the administrative and fairness issues we discussed extensively with respect to consumption taxation still work against its wholesale adoption.

Estate versus inheritance taxation

In another area of tax policy, principles of desert may suggest inheritance taxes as an alternative to our current system of estate and gift taxation. Currently, in the United States we place the focus of our intergenerational transfer taxation on the decedent or donor, while any gifts received are tax free to the recipient or donee. Above a specified threshold, estates and gifts are subject to high rates of taxation. Estate and gift taxes are extremely unpopular as they seem to run against an ingrained American ethos of promoting wealth accumulation and encouraging individual aspirations for success.[33]

Although there is no clear evidence of this point, I would suggest that taxing inheritances does not trigger the same emotional reactions as taxing estates. When we tax an estate, the tax is nominally levied on the same person who ostensibly earned that wealth. From a psychological point of view, this appears to be singling out the same person twice, generating the clear appearance of double-taxation. On the other hand, taxing those who inherit wealth removes the tax one level from those who earned the funds, creating more psychological distance. Taxing a gift made by a donor may in some cases generate the same outcome as if it were taxed when received by a donee, but this need not be the case. Under an inheritance tax, the distribution of gifts would also matter. For example, a graduated, progressive inheritance tax would create incentives to spread the wealth, whereas the conventional estate and gift tax would not.[34]

Consumption versus income taxation

Finally, principles of desert could be used to justify taxes based on consumption rather than income for several different reasons. From a psychological perspective like we discussed for inheritances, the act of consumption is one step removed from the work and effort necessary to earn income. Certainly, income is necessary to consume, but there are intervening decisions, as well as the passage of time, from the initial exertion of effort to earn income to eventual consumption. Our moral intuitions for respecting income that is earned do seem different than the intuitions that would respect consumption, even if the consumption is ultimately financed—immediately or in the future—by the same income. The decision to consume income, rather than save it, breaks the immediate psychological connection between the efforts expended to earn income and the ultimate consumption of that income. Edward McCaffery and James Hines call consumption taxation "the last best hope for progressivity in tax" in that they believe that higher tax rates and more redistribution are possible under consumption taxation.[35]

Here, it is important to choose the right type of consumption tax. In Chapter 3, we discussed a cash-flow consumption tax, which is a postpaid consumption tax that functions like a traditional IRA. A cash-flow consumption tax would ensure that the profligate heir to a fortune would incur tax liability immediately as he or she indulged in consumption but postpone it if they continued to save and invest their funds.

Cash-flow consumption taxes have an important property that is broadly consistent with a theory of desert. Under this type of system, extraordinary returns to capital—that is, those returns above a normal market return—would be taxed fully. For example, if an individual deducted $10,000 from income before computing taxes and invested the money in the stock market, she would be taxed on the full proceeds when the sums were withdrawn. If the value of the stock investment soared beyond normal expectations, the government would share in the extraordinary gains from the investment.

Essentially, the government becomes a silent partner in the original $10,000 investment and shares in gains and losses, with the sharing percentage determined by the tax rate.

Consistent with a desert-motivated tax policy, these windfalls could be taxed with the justification that they were not truly earned. If investment gains beyond a normal return are taxed—even at proportional rates—the result would still be progressive as, by definition, windfalls accrue to the relatively wealthy. Now, under a desert perspective, one could argue that sophisticated investors deserve their extra or windfall returns because of their diligence and effort in their investment activities. While that certainly may be the case, one can also argue that the relative balance of effort versus luck in this case tilts toward the side of luck.

Note that prepaid consumption taxes, such as wage taxes or Roth IRAs do not share this property and should be avoided if the goal is to align wealth with desert. As we discussed in Chapter 3, some clever investors amassed vast fortunes in Roth IRAs which will never be subject to tax. Wage taxation or Roth IRAs do not provide a workable solution to the windfall problem. Similarly certain estate tax strategies that effectively prepay an expected tax liability also run afoul of desert considerations.

Our conjectures about the psychological effects of inheritance versus estate and gift taxes or income versus consumption taxes need to be subject to rigorous empirical tests of the underlying psychology. For example, while it may seem plausible that inheritance taxes are more compatible with equity theory than estate and gift taxes, there are no empirical studies that provide direct evidence on this claim. Nicole Florack and Steven Sheffrin demonstrate that equivalent tax structures from the point of view of economic theory can generate different behavioral reactions in the field.[36] For example, they find that the willingness to take a second job under a wage tax is less than under an economically equivalent consumption tax. Thus, further empirical work is needed to provide a firmer psychological basis for conjectures relating to the psychology of desert taxation.

Concluding Thoughts

Philosophical, economic and popular attitudes toward fairness do not lead us to any tidy conclusions. This is contested terrain and will not lead to a definitive tax policy and generates tax controversies at the most basic level. Tax theorists have worked to incorporate different types of fairness concerns in their models, but the underlying disagreements remain.

Certain types of tax structures may balance effort and incentives to pursue unique opportunities, various types of luck and notions of desert better than others. While there is probably more general support for using taxation to provide a broad safety net, even here there are differences on whether and in what circumstances work should be required for social payments. At the top end, the growth of the billionaire class has challenged our thinking on the role of luck. Our income tax system with its realization requirement does a poor job of managing this issue. In a later chapter, we will return specifically to the potential strategies for taxing the very wealthy.

Notes

1 Sheffrin, *Tax Fairness and Folk Justice.*
2 Mirrlees, "An Exploration in the Theory of Optimal Income Taxation."
3 For example, Murphy and Nagel, *The Myth of Ownership* discuss optimal taxation extensively and Kaplow, *The Theory of Taxation and Public Economics* has used optimal income tax theory to rework the modern theory of public finance.
4 For example, contrast Mankiw et al., "Optimal Taxation in Theory and Practice," versus Diamond and Saez, "The Case for a Progressive Tax: From Basic Research to Policy Recommendations."
5 Mankiw and Weinzierl, "The Optimal Taxation of Height: A Case Study in Utilitarian Income Redistribution."
6 See Weinzierl, "Revisiting the Classical View of Benefit-Based Taxation," and "The Promise of Positive Optimal Taxation: Normative Diversity and a Role for Equal Sacrifice."
7 Saez and Stantcheva, "Generalized Social Marginal Welfare Weights for Optimal Tax Theory."
8 Sher, "Generalized Social Marginal Welfare Weights Imply Inconsistent Comparison of Tax Policy."
9 Fleurbaey and Maniquet, "Optimal Income Tax Theory and Principles of Fairness."
10 Examples of this type of work include Weinzierl, "The Promise of Positive Optimal Taxation: Normative Diversity and a Role for Equal Sacrifice," and Bourguignon and Spadaro, "Tax-Benefit Revealed Social Preferences."
11 Rawls, *A Theory of Justice.*
12 For a recent updated discussion on the veil of ignorance and its implications, see Freeman, "Original Position."
13 Mack, *Libertarianism*, 133.
14 Ibid., See Chapters 2 and 3 for discussions of Hume and Hayek.
15 For a more complete discussion of folk justice, see Sheffrin, *Tax Fairness and Folk Justice*, The book contains references to key psychological studies referred in this chapter.
16 Tyler and Lind, "A Relational Model of Authority in Groups."
17 Sheffrin, *Tax Fairness and Folk Justice*, Chapter 3.
18 Ibid., Chapter 3.
19 Wintour, "Boris Johnson among Record Numbers to Renounce American Citizenship in 2016."
20 Murphy and Nagel, *The Myth of Ownership.*
21 Miller, *Principles of Social Justice.*
22 The origin of this quote is discussed in Sheffrin, "What Role Can Desert Play in Designing Tax Policy," 147.

23 Freiman and Nichols, "Is Desert in the Details?"
24 Ibid., at. 128.
25 Mankiw, "Spreading the Wealth Around: Reflections Inspired by Joe the Plumber."
26 See Singer, "For Top Medical Students, An Attractive Field."
27 They now earn salaries closer to radiologists and cardiologists. See Kaplan, "Average Salaries for Doctors."
28 Nam, "Taxing Option Luck."
29 See Thaler, "Anomalies: The Ultimatum Game," for a discussion.
30 Fehr and Schmidt, "A Theory of Fairness, Competition, and Coordination."
31 Oxoby and Spraggon, "Mine and Yours: Property in Dictator Games."
32 Feinberg, *Who Gets What.*
33 An excellent account of opinion about estate taxes can be found in Graetz and Shapiro, *Death by a Thousand Cuts.*
34 Lily Batchelder, "What Should Society Expect from Heirs? The Case for a Comprehensive Inheritance Tax," presents a detailed proposal and analysis for replacing the estate and gift tax with an inheritance tax.
35 This idea is discussed in McCaffery and Hines, "The Last Best Hope for Progressivity in Tax."
36 Florack and Sheffrin, "Psychological Non-Equivalence of Tax Bases: An Empirical Investigation."

Chapter 6

IS THE TAX SYSTEM RACIALLY BIASED?

A Major Announcement

In December 2021, two high U.S. Treasury officials issued a news release that the Office of Tax Policy had initiated a study to analyze the demographic and racial profile of recipients of a series of economic impact payments delivered by the Internal Revenue Service (IRS) to individuals during the pandemic. Their statement also indicated that this would be the first study in a new initiative to analyze racial equity in the tax system.[1]

From one perspective, this announcement was unremarkable. The federal government often analyzes the demographic and racial composition of recipients of federal programs. The economic impact payments in question were effectively benefit programs. During the pandemic, Congress decided that the IRS was the most appropriate agency to rapidly distribute funds to individuals. If a study had been planned to evaluate the distribution of benefits of rental or housing subsidies provided by the U.S. Department of Housing and Urban Development, the agency would not likely have even bothered to issue an announcement.

But the Treasury announcement was about the racial composition of tax payments, not housing subsidies. As a result, it was highly newsworthy; it represented a triumph for advocates for progressive tax policy. Racial information is not collected on tax forms, nor accounted for in official, published documents, and there has been a reluctance for many government agencies to share data with the IRS and legal prohibitions on the IRS on releasing data to other agencies. The Office of Tax Analysis of the U.S. Treasury, with only rare exceptions, had not previously conducted and published any studies that provided racial information related to the payment and distribution of taxes.[2]

The years leading up to the recent Treasury announcement coincided with a time of growing political focus on racial inequities. Through their writings and presentations, progressive tax scholars in law and public finance lobbied the U.S. Treasury, government agencies and other scholars to pay more attention to race and tax. As an example, the president of the National Tax Association chose the topic "Public Finance and Racism" for the title of his 2020 presidential address.[3] Another provocative paper by a legal scholar raised the question, "Should the IRS Know Your Race: The Challenge of Colorblind Tax Data."[4] A tax law professor, Dorothy Brown, published a well-received trade book, *The Whiteness of Wealth*, which indicted the tax system for contributing to racial wealth inequality.[5] This body of research was stimulated by scholarship published more than a decade ago on critical race theory and taxation.[6]

The new Treasury initiative was quite modest in effect. Their press release did not discuss changing U.S. law to either enable the IRS to collect racial data on tax returns or to relax standards to allow the IRS to share racial data with other agencies. Instead, it discussed employing and refining statistical imputation methods, which are techniques to infer race and ethnicity from other available information. This was not revolutionary; other scholars, independent of the Treasury, have relied on publicly available data to provide insights on the empirical relations of taxes and racial groups.[7]

By endorsing the push for more focus on racial and ethnic data with respect to taxation and committing to publishing official studies, the U.S. Treasury engaged in "expressive tax policy" to signify their intentions, beliefs and values. They signaled to the public, the Congress and other governmental agencies that they were now serious about racial equity in taxation.

This is a major departure in practice. Unlike other governmental agencies whose missions quickly shift with current presidential administrations, the staff of the tax agencies of the Treasury have been careful not to allow politics to intrude on their analyses. This long-standing behavior was based on an institutional belief that politics could potentially interfere with the overall tax collection functions of the agency. To be sure, the commitment to use new statistical methods to analyze race and tax does not in itself compromise the agencies functions, but it does raise questions as to what uses will be made of such data.

The U.S. income tax system is facially neutral in the way the tax code is written. There are no explicit income tax exclusions, deductions or tax differentials directly tied to race or ethnicity. Neither racial nor ethnic information appears on tax returns. With these formal strictures, what type of racial bias can appear in the tax system?

From the legal perspective, discrimination can in principle result from either *disparate treatment*, which is intentional discrimination, or from *disparate impacts* where the consequences of race neutral policies have differential effects on groups. Since the tax system is facially race neutral, there is no intentional discrimination. The key issue is whether it generates disparate impacts across groups and, if so, what, if anything, should be done to address these impacts.

While the distinction between disparate treatment and disparate impacts is helpful in thinking through policies, there can be some challenging boundary issues. For example, lawmakers could write laws with discriminatory intent that are facially neutral. The poll tax for voting would be one example: it applied to all voters, so it was facially neutral, but it was clearly intended to have a differential racial impact. Disparate impacts can sometimes be a potential clue to uncovering disparate treatment.

In this chapter, I begin by presenting the prima facie case why there might be disparate impacts for racial groups from the tax code. The term "disparate impact" has an important legal dimension. There is a rich and evolving legal history of disparate impact analysis in the United States generated by actions of the Congress and the courts. The U.S. Supreme Court has addressed these issues several times over the last fifty years and their decisions and reasoning can help to situate the analysis and potential responses to disparate impacts in the tax code. With this background, I then turn to a more detailed look at the sources and appropriate responses to potential disparate racial impacts in the U.S. tax system.

What Do Existing Data Show?

Although there are no existing data sources that explicitly match tax records with racial and ethnic demographics, other data sources can provide a reasonable assessment of why there may be disparate racial impacts. Racial groups in the United States differ in income, wealth, asset holdings, homeownership and other important characteristics. The U.S. tax system assigns tax liabilities based on these characteristics. Since the tax system is progressive, groups with higher average incomes will, on balance, pay a higher share of their income in taxes. On the other hand, tax preferences or tax expenditures may favor higher-income groups who earn certain types of income, engage in more retirement savings or have a different composition of asset holdings.

There are significant and important economic differences between white and black families in the United States. Based on data compiled from public sources, Thomas Neubig calculates that for 2018, median black family income was 58 percent of white family income, whereas black family wealth was only 13 percent of white family wealth.[8] Group averages of course disguise differences in other variables such as age, family size or the distribution of income, but other research indicates that the striking white–black differences in family wealth holdings persist after controlling for age and for the level of income.[9]

Homeownership and asset holding patterns also differ by race. For middle-aged families, Neubig estimates that the white homeownership rate is 73 percent, while the black homeownership rate is 51 percent. With respect to retirement contributions, 65 percent of whites have either an IRA or a defined benefit plan whereby the corresponding figure for blacks is 44 percent. Perhaps not surprisingly given their respective wealth levels, 61 percent of white families have direct or indirect ownership through financial intermediaries of corporate equity as compared to 34 percent for blacks.[10]

These income and wealth differentials have predictable consequences for differences in tax liabilities. With their higher income, white families would have higher average income tax rates because of the progressivity of the system. This could be partially offset however by several factors. Since white families have more wealth, we would anticipate that they also have more income that is taxed at the lower dividend and capital gains tax rates. In addition, with their higher income and wealth holdings, we would also expect them on average to benefit more from some of the myriad retirement savings incentives. With higher incomes, white families are also more likely to itemize on their tax returns and take advantage of the homeowner's mortgage interest deduction, partial exclusion of gains on owner-occupied housing and charitable contribution deductions.

Using data on tax expenditures by income and census data on white and black incomes, Neubig also estimated the share of tax expenditures flowing to white and black households. For two of the major tax expenditures, the earned income tax credit and the child care credit, black households earned a higher share of the credits than their proportion in the population. This finding is not unexpected as both credits favor lower-income households. On the other hand, the other major tax expenditures, which include the favorable treatment for capital gains, pension savings, health care exclusions, deductions for mortgage interest, charitable contributions and state and local tax payments are tilted toward white households.[11] Individual micro data could provide more refined estimates as well as an assessment of the net effects from progressive tax rates, preferential rates for income from capital and tax expenditures.

Based on years of reports from the Congressional Budget Office, average income tax rates rise with income, despite preferential rates for capital income and tax expenditures. That strongly suggests that with lower average incomes, black households would also have lower average tax rates than white households. Even so, specific tax policies could have differential effects across groups.

The legal literature on disparate impacts can provide insights into how we may wish to think about these differences. It addresses the question of under what circumstances disparate impacts across groups constitute illegal discrimination and, if so, what would be appropriate remedies. To be sure, while illegal discrimination and its potential remedies are not the only points of concern one may have about racial disparities, it is a sound starting point. The compromises and contours of the law also are likely to represent similar judgments in popular sentiment.

Disparate Impact in U.S. Law

As a prelude to our legal discussion, a brief overview of discrimination in U.S. law will be helpful. Racial discrimination is prohibited by the U.S Constitution for government actors and by congressional statutes against both government and private actors. But what counts as discrimination varies definitionally. The U.S. Constitution prohibits intentional discrimination, but not policies that were adopted neutrally but simply result in unequal effects. By contrast, in attempting to combat racial inequality, Congress has targeted certain areas of social life where outcomes, not merely intent, are measured and disparate outcomes must be justified in those areas by business necessity.

The question of whether disparate impacts can constitute evidence of illegal discrimination has been debated at the highest level in the U.S. court system for over fifty years. While there has been considerable controversy over the contours of disparate impact, there are two broad takeaways from its legal history.

First, the U.S. Supreme Court has upheld the use of disparate impact analysis for specific congressionally enacted laws, most frequently in employment and housing matters, but has coupled its approval with restrictions on its use and on the potential remedies for discrimination. However, the Court conversely declined to consider disparate impacts by themselves as evidence to establish violations of equal protection under the U.S. Constitution. As a result, disparate impact analysis needs to be specifically authorized by law and is subject to a variety of restrictions before establishing evidence of discrimination.

Second, the Supreme Court has generally seen disparate impact analysis as a vehicle to break down previous barriers to employment or housing for minorities or to prevent past discrimination from being ossified through current practices. The latest major disparate impact decision in the Supreme Court was the 2015 *Inclusive Communities* decision, which recognized the legitimacy of disparate impact analysis under the Fair Housing Act.[12] One commentator wrote that the Court upheld disparate impact liability "as a targeted 'barrier removal' mechanism rather than a blunt instrument," displacing governmental priorities.[13] In its opinion on *Inclusive Communities*, the

Court also stressed the continuity of its ruling with respect to removing barriers in housing to earlier Court decisions removing barriers to employment.

In the U.S. Supreme Court's first disparate impact case in 1971, *Griggs v. Duke Power,* the Court interpreted Title VII of the 1964 Civil Rights Act as generating the authority to strike down tests used in employment that were not directly job-related. In its decision, the Court used the term "barriers" twice:

> The objective of Congress in the enactment of Title VII is plain from the language of the statute. It was to achieve equality of employment opportunities and remove *barriers* that have operated in the past to favor an identifiable group of white employees over other employees ... What is required by Congress is the removal of artificial, arbitrary, and unnecessary *barriers* to employment when the barriers operate invidiously to discriminate on the basis of racial or other impermissible classification.[14] (Italics added)

Moreover, the Court stated that under the Civil Rights Act, "practices, procedures, or tests neutral on their face, and even neutral in terms of intent, cannot be maintained if they operate to 'freeze' the status quo of prior discriminatory employment practices."[15]

What was not clear from *Griggs v. Duke Power* was whether disparate impact analysis was tied specifically to Title VII of the Civil Rights Act or was a broader strategy that could invalidate other practices without specific statutory provisions. Five years later, the Supreme Court settled this issue in *Washington v. Davis*, where it ruled that disparate impact analysis alone—without evidence of discriminatory intent—could not be used to invalidate governmental practices under the Equal Protection Clause of the Fourteenth Amendment of the U.S. Constitution. Specifically, with respect to the Equal Protection Clause: "Disproportionate impact is not irrelevant, but it is not the sole touchstone of an invidious racial discrimination forbidden by the Constitution."[16]

In its opinion, the Court also took the opportunity to issue a stern advisory as to the broad use of disparate impact analysis, one that also previewed future Court concerns and potential policy concerns about unanticipated consequences.

> A rule that a statute designed to serve neutral ends is nevertheless invalid, absent compelling justification, if in practice it benefits or burdens one race more than another would be far reaching and would raise serious questions about, and perhaps invalidate, a whole range of tax,

welfare, public service, regulatory, and licensing statutes that may be more burdensome to the poor and to the average black than to the more affluent white.[17]

Note that tax was listed first in the areas that could be potentially complicated by disparate impact analysis.

Several Supreme Court cases have also highlighted challenges with the use of disparate impact analysis. In some cases, remedies for disparate impact claims can raise significant difficulties, because they may require the government or an employer to use potentially illegal race-conscious methods. In other cases, remedies may invalidate otherwise reasonable government policies.[18]

The history of the *Inclusive Communities* case portrays the limitations that the Court has placed on the use of disparate impact analysis, as well as some of the practical difficulties in implementing the standard. This case involved the allocation of federal tax credits for low-income housing. The Texas agency responsible had allocated these credits to inner-city neighborhoods of high poverty and blight. They were challenged in court by a nonprofit, the Inclusive Communities Project, on the grounds that the agency allocation had disproportionately allocated the credits toward black inner-city neighborhoods and not to predominantly white suburban neighborhoods (disparate impact). The nonprofit argued that this allocation of tax credits perpetuated patterns of racial segregation.

Justice Anthony Kennedy wrote the majority opinion, which found that the relevant language of the Fair Housing Act permitted disparate impact liability, emphasizing as we noted above "barrier removal." Justice Kennedy, however, also placed limits on its use. A practice should not be found to be discriminatory merely because it caused statistical disparities. Before a valid claim could be made, the plaintiffs had to establish "robust causality," that is, the practice in question caused the observed disparities. Defendants have leeway to offer a justification. Neither the law nor courts should be in the business of second-guessing legitimate governmental actions—a defense analogous to business necessity for governments. Policies, whether private or governmental, should not be ruled discriminatory unless they are "artificial, arbitrary, and unnecessary barriers."[19] Moreover, "Courts should avoid interpreting disparate-impact liability to be so expansive as to inject racial considerations into every housing decision."[20] Finally, remedies for disparate impact must adhere strictly to constitutional norms and avoid discriminatory remedies.

In its decision, the Court decided that disparate impact liability could in principle be established under the Fair Housing Act and sent the case back to the lower courts. When a Texas district court in 2016 evaluated the claim with new guidance from the Supreme Court, they found that the Inclusive Communities Project had *not* met the burdens required by the Supreme Court and dismissed their claim. In particular, the district court found that the plaintiff had not identified a specific policy used in awarding tax credits that caused the disparity of the location of low-income housing and that the nonprofit had also not identified a specific barrier the court could remove.

This brief review of some of the legal history associated with disparate impact analysis provides several important insights. Unless authorized by statute, disparate impact analysis cannot establish liability; evidence of disparate treatment will be required. Successful disparate impact claims have been associated with areas, such as employment or housing, where there have been at some point long-standing discriminatory practices. The strongest rationale for using disparate impact analysis is to break down segregation. A defense by an employer or the government against a disparate impact claim can rely on business necessity or a legitimate governmental purpose; only arbitrary and artificial policies that create barriers do not meet this standard. Even when allowed under statute, the purported discriminatory policy must also meet a causality standard linking the defendant's policy to outcomes. Remedies for disparate impact must themselves meet strict standards, especially about race-conscious solutions. The intricate balancing act and strict requirements that the Court prescribes in the employment and housing cases will bear on our assessment of disparate impacts in taxation.

Taxation and Disparate Impacts

In the law, controversies about disparate impact hinge on whether they constitute illegal discrimination and, if so, what remedies might be appropriate. In taxation, our concerns are broader—is there evidence that disparate impacts cause outcomes that fail to meet our normative standards? Other factors other than illegal discrimination may be important. Despite these differences, the insights from the legal literature are helpful in developing normative standards and evaluating specific tax provisions.

One important difference between taxation and the legal areas where disparate impact analysis has been most extensively applied—housing and employment—there are no obvious historical legacies of discrimination to remove through changes in tax policy. In principle, one could make a case that a particular tax policy created barriers to advancement or progress. As discussed above, poll taxes, which were designed to keep minorities from the voting booth, would be one example of a tax policy that creates barriers. Poll taxes, however, were deemed unconstitutional by the Supreme Court in 1966.

Moreover, they are not the type of taxes highlighted by critics of the current tax system.

Most of the existing discussion in the tax literature focuses on purely distributional patterns of taxation and the burdens and benefits of our current tax structure. It is a question of "who gets what." Some scholars have attempted to go further: Dorothy Brown has argued that the tax system bears major responsibility for the relative income or wealth disparities between blacks and whites in the United States.[21] Would distributional outcomes from taxation by themselves constitute barriers to, say, housing integration? This is unlikely, as a myriad of other factors—economic, educational demographic and overt discriminatory policies all contribute to black–white income differentials.

Aside from distributional concerns, there may be important administrative or procedural issues with respect to taxation that affect race. For example, groups may be treated differently in audit settings or even in tax court proceedings by judges.[22] At the local level, property tax assessments and appeals might also have a racial or ethnic component.[23] Distinguishing between the effects of income and race for understanding the disposition of income tax audits, court proceedings or property tax administration is challenging, but it is a subject worth examining. Nonetheless, much of the discussion on race and taxation has focused on distributional issues.

Before analyzing specific tax policies, it is important to step back and address some key measurement issues. Do we want to analyze the entire fiscal environment, with both taxes and spending? If we just focus on taxes, what level of aggregation should be used? Should we look at the impact of all tax provisions, a small group of provisions or at specific tax policies one-by-one? Finally, in measuring tax expenditures, what baseline should we use: a pure income tax, a pure consumption tax or our current hybrid system?

Measurement issues

Taxes are created to finance government spending, but spending also has disparate impacts across groups. This insight raises the question of whether we want to conduct a full fiscal analysis with both taxes and spending or restrict our attention to taxes. How we define "taxes" and "spending" will also matter.

The results of any study will be sensitive to all these choices. To illustrate this point, let us start with an example why it matters how we define taxes and spending. Consider the recent analysis of the distribution of taxes in *The Triumph of Injustice* by Emmanuel Saez and Gabriel Zucman.[24] In their broad examination of both federal and state and local taxes, they surprisingly found that the average tax rate across households was reasonably constant across income groups. In arriving at this conclusion, they did not include the earned income tax credit, which is a subsidy (or negative tax) for low-income workers. Their rationale for their unorthodox choice was that the earned income tax credit was refundable—that is, individuals would receive it whether they had any tax liability to offset. Therefore, they deemed it a spending program and not a tax program.

Government agencies, such as the Congressional Budget Office, differ from Saez and Zucman and deem refundable credits to be negative taxes which offset other taxes paid. Refundable credits are important. In 2021, the child care credit was temporarily expanded and made refundable. The credit was also phased out slowly as income rose, so households filing joint returns could earn up to $400,000 before losing the credit entirely. Proponents of the child care credit sometimes referred to it as a middle-class tax cut indicating that they believed refundable credits were simply negative taxes.

With respect to assessing disparate impact, the treatment of refundable credit is important. As we saw from Neubig's estimates, black households have lower average income and receive a higher proportion of the earned income tax credit than their share of total households. Thus, how we classify refundable credits would clearly affect calculations of tax expenditures by racial group.

Going beyond definitional issues of spending and taxes, it is also important to decide whether we consider them in combination. For example, federal taxes fund the Supplemental Nutrition Assistance Program and health insurance subsidies under the Affordable Care Act. Both these programs provide subsidies to low or lower-middle income households. There are many other examples. States use their taxes, sometimes with federal help, to fund unemployment insurance payments. Social Security payments are based on wages, but the fraction of wages that Social Security payments replace declines as wages increase. Once we account for these types of social spending, the distribution of net fiscal benefits shifts toward lower- and middle-income households. Including these spending programs would also affect our calculations of disparate impacts.

If we restrict the analysis to conventional definitions of taxes (including refundable credits) and do not take government spending into account, we still must decide how to measure federal effective tax rates. The most straightforward way would be to first add all types of income together, including wages, interest (both taxable and tax exempt), dividends and realized capital gains. Ideally, we also would want to measure income before allowing exclusions for retirement payments and health insurance. As we discuss in Chapter 7, some recent work has also included retained earnings of corporations as they can be seen as income accruing households, the ultimate owners of corporations.

This ensures parallel treatment for business entities that pass-through their earnings directly, such as partnerships, S-Corporations and individual proprietorships.[25] Once we have this total for income, we divide it into total federal taxes paid, which would ideally include individual and corporate income taxes as well as payroll taxes. The result would be a comprehensive measure of effective tax rates by income class.

Various government agencies have prepared calculations in this spirit, although not including retained earnings of corporations in income. Aggregate analysis along these lines by the Congressional Budget Office show that effective tax rates rise consistently with income.[26] The only exception in their work is at the very top of the income distribution. The CBO reports that the top .01 percent of taxpayers have a slightly lower tax rate than the other taxpayers in the top 0.1 percent, although the difference is small.[27]

Since average incomes are lower for black Americans and white Americans, these findings strongly suggest that the *overall average effective tax rate* would be less for black Americans. Within each racial group, effective tax rates would rise with income. More detailed analysis involving imputations or potential matching, as suggested by the U.S. Treasury's new initiatives, would be required to spell out more nuanced features for the pattern of effective tax rates. Differences in family structures, asset holdings and other socioeconomic differences could have some effects. For example, to the extent that black households hold fewer assets than white households at the same income level, they may have higher effective taxes at those levels of income, as capital income is subject to lower tax rates than wage income. Despite these differences, the average effective tax rates of different racial or ethnic groups will almost surely track their differences in income.

Much of the recent discussion over racial differences in taxation has focused less on aggregate average effective tax rates and more on specific provisions in the tax code. The three aspects of the tax code that have been discussed the most are: the advantages of joint versus single filing, the home mortgage interest deduction and the preferences for income from capital.

Tax expenditures and disparate impacts

For each specific tax code provision, we can ask four questions. First, why might there be a difference between races with respect to the specific tax provision and is it likely to be robust? Second, if there is a difference, can it be concretely linked to racial discrimination in the present or sometime in the past? Third, is there a legitimate public policy rationale for this provision? Finally, tying our analysis to the concerns that animate the legal discussion, would removal of the tax provision help reduce barriers that have been created by past discriminatory patterns?

Marriage penalties

In her book *The Whiteness of Wealth*, Dorothy Brown argued that overall differences in filing status for income taxes for blacks and whites in the United States likely have disparate racial impacts.[28] She recounted that as a young professional she paid less tax than her parents who earned a similar total income. The difference arose because of a marriage penalty that prevailed at that time.

Marriage penalties are defined as the additional tax that a married couple would pay in taxes on their jointly filed tax return relative to the total taxes that would be paid if each of the partners filed as individuals and were not required to file a joint return. Marriage subsidies are defined analogously. Marriage penalties or subsidies can arise because the tax system tries to balance three distinct principles. The first is neutrality for couples, meaning couples with the same total income should pay the same in taxes, regardless of the composition of the household income between partners. The second is tax progressivity—higher income individuals should pay taxes at a higher average rate. The third is that there should be no change in tax liabilities upon marriage—that is, there should be marriage neutrality.[29]

Unfortunately, these three principles are not compatible with one another. With a progressive rate structure, a married couple filing jointly with one high earner and one low earner can effectively split the income between them and reduce their overall tax burden within a progressive tax system. It will generally be the case that couples with more equal incomes will be relatively disadvantaged—either facing higher penalties or lower subsidies—than couples with more unequal incomes.[30]

Joint filing with a separate tax set of tax rates was instituted to avoid a thorny problem of differences between the states in their property laws. Some states were community property states where, the U.S. Supreme Court ruled in 1930, couples could share their income. That meant that if one person in the household was the owner of financial assets, they could allocate some of the income generated by the asset to their partner as well as their wages, thereby effectively splitting the income within the household. On the other hand, residents of noncommunity property states did not have this luxury. To avoid penalizing this latter group, Congress in 1948 passed legislation allowing all married couples to combine their income for tax purposes—their tax liability was computed as twice the tax liability on half their joint income. This was a very generous marriage bonus, which Congress reduced in 1969, thereby creating the first possibility of a marriage penalty.[31] By adjusting the tax brackets for joint filers versus single filers, Congress can affect the marriage penalty or subsidy. The 2017 tax bill eliminated most marriage penalties but, of course, did not eliminate differential subsidies.

Dorothy Brown has argued that black households are more likely to have two equal earners than white families and would be more likely to face a marriage penalty or smaller bonus. In her view, even if these differences are small in any one year, they could cumulate and cause wealth differences over time. In *The Whiteness of Wealth*, she provided some evidence on earnings data from the 2010 census data suggesting that, under the tax law prevailing at that time, there were differential tax effects of marriage by race.[32] Whether a differential pattern persist today under the current tax law would have to be analyzed with contemporary data. With the rise of female labor force participation over the last fifty years, changing gender representation in colleges and professional schools, rapidly evolving marriage trends for both black and white families, coupled with significant changes in the tax law, it is not clear what the precise patterns of penalties and bonuses would be today. Nor would such a pattern necessarily be stable. One complexity is that other factors, such as the number of children and the structure of benefit programs such as the earned income tax credit, also affect the total calculation of the tax benefits to marriage. Again, a definitive answer would require more detailed analysis of tax data combined with imputation of demographic and racial information.

Looking at this from the perspective of the Supreme Court's jurisprudence on disparate impact, joint filing was instituted to avoid discrepancies in taxation between taxpayers in community property versus noncommunity property states. It was not created specifically for any racial purpose, so there was no presumption of disparate treatment. Although joint filing is certainly not the only possible system of taxation—other developed countries such as Canada and the United Kingdom require independent filing—joint filing has a legitimate policy rationale for the United States with its federalist system and respect for the legal framework in individual states. Finally, eliminating joint filing would not eliminate any obvious racial barriers in employment, housing or other areas of economic life. Joint filing may or may not have differences across racial groups, but these differences would not constitute racial discrimination under our current constitutional legal framework.

Mortgage interest deduction

A second issue that has been raised frequently is the home mortgage interest deduction. As we discussed in Chapter 2, the mortgage interest deduction is a classic tax expenditure, as interest costs are deductible by homeowners without imputed rental income being included. The 2017 tax law, however, sharply reduced the use of the mortgage interest deduction because fewer taxpayers now itemize their deductions. Nonetheless, it continues to provide some potential benefits to higher-income households. In the past, these benefits may have been spread more broadly across the larger number of taxpayers who itemized their deductions, but even that claim is debatable. To the extent that the mortgage interest deduction increased the demand for housing and raised its price, its benefit may have been diluted for taxpayers claiming the mortgage interest deduction and penalized nonitemizing homeowners.

Although the reach of the mortgage interest deduction may be somewhat limited today, it is clearly a tax benefit that is within an area of the economy that has a long history of racial discrimination, stemming from both private and public actions. As Richard Rothstein described in his book *The Color of Law*, the Federal Housing Administration, dating back to the Great Depression, furthered housing segregation efforts by refusing to insure mortgages in and near black neighborhoods. At the same time, it was subsidizing builders who were mass-producing large housing tracts for whites, coupled with the requirement that none of the houses be sold to blacks.[33] Racial covenants in property deeds were common in the United States and had long-ranging effects despite a 1948 U.S. Supreme Court decision that racial covenants could not be legally enforced.[34] Although there are no formal legal barriers to homeownership today, the history of discrimination and segregation in housing casts a long shadow.

There has been extensive work documenting and trying to explain the significant black–white homeownership differential, which reached 30.1 percentage points in 2017. One recent study found that controlling both for personal factors such as income, marital status, education and credit scores as well as location-specific factors by metropolitan region, such as housing supply, affordability and existing patterns of racial segregation, explained much of the difference but these factors could still not account for 17 percent of the gap. The author found that more highly segregated metropolitan districts had higher white homeowner rates. The study offered a variety of other possible explanations for the remaining unexplained differences, including "parental wealth, information access, housing supply challenges, or the vestiges of policies that have made it difficult for black households to obtain homes."[35] Based on this work, it is highly likely that black households would be less likely to benefit from the mortgage interest deduction than white households, even after controlling for income and other factors.

However, eliminating the mortgage interest deduction would not directly or even indirectly tackle the black–white homeownership gap or help break down vestiges from past discrimination. As it is currently structured, it is a general policy that provides subsidies to higher-income households, both black and white, to purchase housing. Tax policy scholars would generally welcome its elimination or restructuring it as a credit—over the objection of the housing lobby and some existing homeowners currently taking the deduction—but its elimination would not be a significant factor impacting housing policy. Thus, while the mortgage interest deduction does touch on an area that has been implicated by past discrimination, a tax reform would only tangentially affect the housing market.

Capital income preferences

As we have discussed throughout the book, through exclusions, reduced tax rates and opportunities for deferrals, capital income is taxed at much lower rates than ordinary income. Since the empirical evidence suggests that white households have higher wealth levels than black households at any level of income, the preferential taxation of capital income would be more beneficial to white households. However, since wealth holdings—and thus the benefits of tax preferences for capital income—are highly concentrated, it is not clear how large the total racial differential would be. At high levels of income—say over $10 million per year—it is not obvious that black households differ substantially from white households in terms of wealth holding and the benefits from capital income subsidies. For the median household, however, it is much more likely the case that white households would benefit more from this preference. Again, we need new data sources to answer this question combining tax, demographic and racial information. But assuming there is an overall tilt towards white households, how should we think about this?

If a Haig–Simons income tax is our reference point, then preferences for capital income would be tax expenditures, which in this case would be steered to high income and, for the sake of argument, white households. However, we live under a hybrid tax system, split between income and consumption taxation. Under a consumption tax, capital income would be more lightly taxed and some of the tax advantages of preferential capital income taxation would be the norm. Reduced taxation for capital income would no longer be a tax preference but part of the overall tax system.

As we discussed in Chapter 3, the United States has forged an uneasy and complex compromise between income and consumption taxation, weighing efficiency, fairness and administrative concerns. Racial issues did not directly enter this debate—the primary focus was on overall distributional fairness between high income, high wealth individuals and others. To be sure some of the normative discussions focused on the relative fairness of taxation of high- versus low-saving households, but even that discussion was second order compared to the broader efficiency versus fairness debate.

While at single point in time, increasing taxes on capital income might tilt the balance of taxes toward black households, there could be offsetting dynamic effects. Some black small business organizations have argued that reducing preferences for capital income could potentially have adverse long-run effects on wealth accumulation for minority communities.[36] They argue that reducing tax preferences for capital income would pull up the drawbridge before they have had a chance to cross. If their view is correct, raising taxes on capital income would create, not destroy existing barriers.

Concluding Thoughts

With respect to the income tax, the fundamental issue is whether differences between groups arising from a facially neutral tax system rise to a level of discrimination that normatively should be addressed by policies that are consistent with the legal and constitutional requirements for government action. The legal framework that has developed around disparate impacts has carefully distinguished between statistical differences that may emerge as the outcomes of legitimate public policies from those outcomes stemming from policies that reinforce or create barriers or perpetuate past discriminatory practices. In the income tax area, the most common tax preferences singled out for potential adverse impacts—joint versus individual filing, the mortgage interest deduction and the preferential taxation of income from wealth—all have some legitimate policy arguments to support them, and these provisions do not by themselves create any social barriers. Each policy has been repeatedly debated vigorously on general tax policy grounds. For these specific income tax provisions racial differences in outcomes are at best likely to be secondary considerations in any debate.

There may be other tax policy areas where racial issues play a more important social role. Consider the property tax system in California introduced in 1978 with Proposition 13. In this system, property is only reassessed fully to current market values when it is sold. If a property is not sold, the property's assessed value—and the taxes on the property—can only increase by two percent a year. This has the consequences of reducing household mobility because selling an existing property and moving to a new one will trigger an increase in property taxation.[37] This reduction in social mobility could adversely affect integration and potentially exclude residents from moving to more desirable communities.[38] The U.S. Supreme Court in 1992, however, upheld Proposition 13 as a justifiable public policy decision by the voters to provide certainty in taxation as well as to potentially preserve communities.[39]

Perhaps in today's environment one may wish to rethink that decision, balancing the desire to preserve communities with the removal of social barriers.

Proponents of shining a racial lens on tax policy have achieved an important expressive milestone with the announcement by the U.S. Treasury that it would embark on new studies and develop new institutional capacities for future studies. But even if these future studies find statistical differences between groups based on income, age, asset holdings or other factors, changing long-standing tax policies with alternative, facially neutral policies that meet constitutional standards for government action will be an exceedingly difficult challenge.

Unlike some other areas of tax policy, there are minimal major empirical disputes. Rather the clash in political perspectives stems from different philosophical and legal orientations toward disparate racial outcomes. These deeper differences underlie the tax policy controversies.

Notes

1 U.S. Department of Treasury, "Advancing Equity Analysis in Tax Policy."
2 Bearer-Friend, "Should the IRS Know Your Race?" The Treasury's Office of Tax Analysis most recently released a paper on tax expenditures and race in January 2023.
3 Gale, "Public Finance and Racism."
4 Bearer-Friend, "Should the IRS Know Your Race?"
5 Brown, Dorothy, *The Whiteness of Wealth.*
6 An early influential paper was Moran and Whitford, "A Black Critique of the Internal Revenue Code."
7 For example, Neubig, "Disparate Racial Impact: Tax Expenditure Reform Needed."
8 Ibid., Table 1.
9 McIntosh, et al., "Examining the Black-White Wealth Gap."
10 Data in this paragraph is from Neubig, "Disparate Racial Impact: Tax Expenditure Reform Needed," Table 2.
11 Ibid., Neubig, "Disparate Racial Impact: Tax Expenditure Reform Needed," Figure 2.
12 The case is *Texas Department of Housing and Community Affairs v. Inclusive Communities Project.*
13 Seicshnaydre, "Disparate Impact and the Limits of Local Discretion After Inclusive Communities," 664.
14 *Griggs vs. Duke Power Co.* 401 U.S. 424 (1971) Page 401 U.S. 429.
15 Ibid., Page 401 U.S. 430.
16 *Washington Davis* 426 U.S. 229 (1976) Page 426 U.S. 242.
17 *Washington Davis* 426 U.S. 229 (1976) Page 426 U.S. 248.
18 See, for example, the discussion in *Ricci v. DeStefano* 557 US 557 (2009) Page 557 U.S. 558.
19 *Texas Department of Housing and Community Affairs v. Inclusive Communities Project.* Page 576 U.S. 521.

20 *Texas Department of Housing and Community Affairs v. Inclusive Communities Project.* Page 576 U.S. 543.

21 Brown, *The Whiteness of Wealth.*

22 This is a point that been emphasized by Dean, "Filing While Black: The Casual Racism of the Tax Law."

23 See, for example, Atuahene, "Taxed Out: Illegal Property Tax Assessments and the Epidemic of Tax Foreclosures in Detroit."

24 Saez and Zucman, *The Triumph of Injustice.*

25 See Auten and Splinter, "Income Inequality in the United States: Using Tax Data to Measure Long-Term Trends."

26 Congressional Budget Office, "The Distribution of Household Income, 2018," 4.

27 Ibid., Exhibit 10.

28 Brown, *The Whiteness of Wealth.*

29 There is an extensive literature on marriage penalties. For a clear discussion, see Alm et al., "Policy Watch: The Marriage Penalty."

30 See Pomerleau, "Understanding the Marriage Penalty and Bonus," and Isaac, "Lecture Notes on Income Taxation," for updated patterns. If one is willing to achieve progressivity with a flat tax rate and a refundable demogrant, you can avoid this issue, see Hemel, "Beyond the Marriage Tax Trilemma."

31 Rosen, "The Marriage Tax is Down but Not Out."

32 Brown, *The Whiteness of Wealth,* Chapter 1 Tables 1.2-1.5.

33 Rothstein, *The Color of Law.*

34 U.S. Supreme Court case *Shelley vs Kraemer* 334 U.S. 1 (1948).

35 Choi, "Breaking Down the Black-White Homeownership Gap."

36 Sylvester, "Congress should not Raise Taxes on Black-Owned Business."

37 O'Sullivan, Sheffrin, and Sexton, *Property Taxes and Tax Revolts: The Legacy of Proposition 13.*

38 Sarkar and Rosenthal, "Exclusionary Taxation."

39 *Nordlinger v Hahn* 505 U.S. 1 (1992).

Chapter 7

HOW CAN WE TAX THE
VERY WEALTHY?

In the aftermath of the global financial crisis, the Occupy Wall Street move-ment caught the world's attention with their occupation of Zuccotti Park in lower Manhattan. Their seizure of the park in September 2011 and repeated skirmishes with authorities determined to remove them focused attention on the core idea of their protest: growing inequality throughout the world. Government actions to fight the financial crisis, such as bailouts for large financial firms attracted their ire. Their slogan "We are the 99%" turned into a rallying cry for forces opposed to inequality and highlighted the gains in income and wealth that had accrued to the top 1 percent of the income distribution.

The belief that the top 1 percent had gained an increasingly growing share of economic income had reached popular consciousness and was highlighted by left-leaning think tanks such as the Center on Budget and Policy Priorities in the United States.[1] These beliefs helped drive the Occupy movement. But where did this belief about the top 1 percent originate? As is the case with other radical movements, the sentiments driving their actions came from scholarly research. This time, however, it was not the product of a German immigrant toiling over data in the British Museum, but instead arose from collaborations between academic scholars at elite institutions in Paris and Berkeley, California.

Thomas Piketty of the University of Paris and Emmanuel Saez of Berkeley had obtained access to confidential tax data from the Internal Revenue Service (IRS) which allowed them to document the share of income reported on tax returns over long periods of time. Their first study was published in one of the top economic journals and then regularly updated.[2] A typical find-ing of their work was that the share of income earned by the top 1 percent increased from 10 percent in 1960 to 21.5 percent by 2014, more than dou-bling. To put it another way, 1 percent of taxpayers were earning one-fifth of all the income in the United States.

The popular focus on inequality increased after the Occupy movement in 2014 with the publication of Piketty's best-selling book, *Capital in the Twenty-First Century*.[3] This also led to an increased focus on tax policy and inspired candidates in the 2016 presidential campaign to propose ways to tax the rich.

Recent scholarship discussed below, however, has cast some doubt on the core Piketty–Saez findings about the growth of the income share of the top 1 percent and the overall change in income inequality in the United States. Nonetheless, as we have highlighted throughout the book, modern tax systems do a relatively poor job of reaching the truly rich. The requirement that income needs to be realized before it can be subject to tax makes it difficult to tax the relatively small number of very top earners at the highest reaches of the top 1 percent.

This chapter begins with recent work that re-examines changes in the distribution of income and why the striking findings of Piketty–Saez potentially may give an inaccurate picture of changes in the distribution of income over time. It then turns to the history of taxing the rich, noting that major changes have only occurred around wars but can persist for some time thereafter.

I then turn to alternative ways to tax appreciation in assets, the source of great income and wealth, including both through wealth taxation and income taxation. Wealth taxation has had only limited success, has been on the decline in Europe and faces potential constitutional obstacles in the United States. There are other income-related options for taxing appreciation of property, but they all will require fundamental changes in basic principles of income taxation, especially the realization principle. The current estate and gift tax can be reformed to better target the fortunes of the ultrawealthy and plug some evident loopholes. Finally, there is one relatively straightforward change to the tax system that could potentially accomplish these goals—ending the step-up in basis of assets at death.

What About the Top 1 Percent?

The starting point for the recent scholarly research on inequality is the use of administrative tax date from the IRS by Piketty and Saez, and more recently with another coauthor Gabriel Zucman. Tax data provide more insight into the income of the rich than typical survey data which provide little detail at the very top of the income distribution. But tax data have their own problems. Two government economists, Gerald Auten of the Treasury Department and David Splinter of the Joint Committee on Taxation, carefully examined the tax data and took a fresh look at the conventional wisdom on what the tax data could reveal.[4] After making some needed adjustments, they found much smaller changes in the distribution of income accruing to the top 1 percent than Piketty and Saez. Their best estimate was that the shares rose from 11 percent in 1962 to 13.8 percent in 2014 (compared to the original Piketty–Saez numbers of 10 to 21.5 percent). Moreover, the Piketty–Saez–Zucman estimates do not include any of the many government cash transfers to individuals, despite the increasing importance over time in these transfers. Once Auten and Splinter adjusted for government transfers (while still accounting for federal taxes paid), they found virtually no change in the top 1 percent income share. They estimated that the after-tax, after-transfer income share of the top 1 percent was 8.5 percent in 1962 and 8.8 percent in 2014. By this measure, the share going to the top 1 percent barely moved over that fifty-year period.

Why are there such dramatic differences between the most recent estimates from Piketty, Saez and Gabriel Zucman, and the estimates from Auten and Splinter? As Auten and Splinter point out, there have been important changes in tax law and demographics over the last fifty years. During this period, the 1986 Tax Reform Act changed the incentives of the rich to report income on their personal tax returns. In addition, marriage rates declined primarily in lower-income brackets, increasing the number of filing units at lower-income levels.

According to Auten and Splinter, both changes falsely inflated the true share of income accruing to the top 1 percent. With more filing units at lower-income levels, the top 1 percent of the population mechanically was now comprised taxpayers who were higher up in the income distribution than previously. Auten and Splinter first adjusted the data to make the data comparable over time. They made a similar adjustment for the increase in tax returns filed by dependents of taxpayers that were induced by changes in the tax law in 1986.

The many tax law changes in the 1986 Tax Reform Act also impacted the measured share of income of the top 1 percent. The reform lowered marginal tax rates substantially and importantly limited the ability of high-income taxpayers to shelter income by new provisions, which included limiting losses on rental income and other types of passive or investment income. These changes curtailed the then burgeoning tax shelter industry. Taxpayers decreased their use of shelters and, with lower tax rates, reported more of their true economic income on their returns. While this economic income was present prior to the 1986 act, it was not being reported on individual returns.

Another major change in the 1986 act was to encourage smaller corporations to change their status from the traditional C corporation regime, in which corporations pay a separate corporate tax and can retain earnings and not pay them immediately to shareholders, to an S corporation regime, which, for tax purposes, pass through their income to their owners as the income is earned. More income from S corporations thus showed up directly on individual returns after 1986.

Auten and Splinter adjust both for the inability to shelter income through losses after the passage of the 1986 act and the change in corporate form leading to more corporate income appearing directly on individual returns. To make this latter adjustment, they remove realized capital gains from individual returns but add back in corporate earnings that they impute to individuals. In their view, without making these adjustments, the income of the top 1 percent would be understated in the 1960s and 1970s, when income could be sheltered through losses or retained in corporate form. One indication that these adjustments are important is that even the Piketty–Saez–Zucman estimates only show large increases in the top 1 percent share starting in the 1990s, after the passage of the 1986 act.

The Auten–Splinter adjustments reduce the change in pretax income of the top 1 percent compared to Piketty–Saez–Zucman. But they also point out that transfer payments to individuals increased dramatically from 5 percent to 16 percent of national income between 1960 and 2019. Since these transfers are directed at lower- and middle-income taxpayers, adjusting for transfers will reduce the share of resources accruing to the top 1 percent. Finally, since the tax system is progressive, adjusting for taxes paid will produce more equal after-tax incomes. With all these adjustments, Auten and Splinter radically reorient our perspectives on the share of income of the top 1 percent.

One word of caution—while tax data are imperfect for the reasons we highlighted, there are several alternative ways to adjust the data to make them comparable over time. Auten and Splinter provide some robustness checks on their methods and provide extended justifications for their method, but scholars, including Piketty, Saez and Zucman, can and do disagree on whether certain adjustments are the most appropriate. Note also that the debate between these two camps of economic statisticians focused on the top 1 percent. But recent interest—as exemplified by the *Pro-Publica* study of billionaires we discussed in Chapter 1—has shifted more to the extremes of the income distribution—the top fraction of the 1 percent.

Our History of Taxing the Rich

When will societies decide to raise taxes on the rich? Political scientists Kenneth Scheve and David Stasavage (hereafter referred to as SS) examined this question carefully for more than 150 years for twenty countries for which they had comprehensive data.[5] They focused on the top statutory rate of taxation—that is, the official tax bracket that applied at the highest level of incomes. Although statutory rates may not capture the true tax burden facing the rich because of exclusions and deductions, they do provide an indication of a society's intention to tax the extraordinarily rich.

A glance at the data for the twenty countries in their sample, which includes most of Europe and the United States, shows that average top statutory income tax rate shot up during World War I to nearly 40 percent, declined after the war, climbed briefly during the Great Depression, but then exceeded 60 percent during World War II. After this war, average rates remained high for a considerable period, but then began to fall and now average less than 40 percent.

The experience in the United States is comparable to the global average. Top statutory rates rose to 77 percent during World War I, fell after the war and then rose during the later years in the 1930s and during World War II, reaching as high as 94 percent. After the war, top rates remained at 91 percent through the 1950s and, starting with tax cuts in the Kennedy Administration in the early 1960s, top rates gradually fell to 50 percent in 1982. The Tax Reform Act of 1986 brought the top rate down to 28 percent, but that low rate only lasted a few years. Since 1993, the top statutory income tax rate in the United States has ranged between 35 and 39.6 percent.

As political scientists, SS were interested in trying to explain this pattern and what drove the period of high statutory rates. They considered several hypotheses. Could the increase in the universal suffrage drive the higher rates, as lower- and middle-class voters tried to redistribute money away from the rich? Do increases in inequality—as we may have experienced in recent years—trigger higher statutory rates to make the distribution of income more equal? Neither of these hypotheses fit the data. The timing of universal suffrage across countries was not related to increases in top statutory tax rates, nor did changes in inequality drive tax rate increases—although there was some evidence that tax rate increases did dampen inequality.

Since the data suggest that tax increases occurred during the major world wars, perhaps the key to understanding the data lie there. SS offer a specific hypothesis, which they term the "compensatory theory," arguing that the sharp increases in top tax rates during the major wars were designed to compensate the rest of the society, whose sons were mobilized to serve and sometimes die in battle. In other words, high statutory tax rates were the solution to the problems posed by the differential burdens it placed on groups within the society in fighting these major wars.

Their most persuasive evidence in favor of this hypothesis compared tax rate increases in countries that mobilized during World War I and countries that did not mobilize. The countries that did not mobilize did raise their top rates during the war by 9.7 percentage points. But the countries that mobilized raised them by 59.7 percentage points. The difference between the two increases (the difference-in-differences) by 48 points and is a strong indicator that mobilizations and the unfair burdens they imposed were the key to understanding increases in top statutory rates. At the ninetieth percentile of the income distribution, the difference-in-differences was a mere 3.8 percentage points. The emphasis therefore was on taxing the extreme rich. Similar patterns were observed in inheritance tax rates across countries.

Since World War II and the Korean conflict, the nature of wars has changed. Mass mobilizations in most Western or European countries are no longer used to fight wars. Many countries, like the United States, have volunteer armies, and sophisticated technologies—drones, cruise missiles and hypersonic aircraft—have substituted for raw manpower. Under these circumstances, there is no longer the need for high top statutory rates to compensate the lower- and middle-class for their wartime sacrifices. As a result, the prospect for future increases in top statutory rates according to SS are low. Without the extraordinary wartime experiences from the days of mass mobilization, the fight over statutory rates will remain in the political trenches, pitting those who desire more progressivity against those who worry more about the adverse economic incentives caused by high rates.

While SS do provide solid evidence for their theories, there are several open questions. In the United States, for example, top statutory rates were increased sharply before World War II by President Franklin Roosevelt, which accompanied his rhetoric attacking "economic royalists." Moreover, after World War II, top statutory rates remained over 90 percent until 1964. Neither the rise nor persistence of top statutory rates are consistent with the compensatory theory. In their defense one could argue that in the United States effective tax rates for the rich diverged from statutory rates. While this is likely true, SS claimed support for their compensatory theory with tests on statutory rates.

Tax historian Ajay Mehrota raised other concerns.[6] He pointed out that both in the United Kingdom and the United States, progressive politics prevailed prior to World War I. There were historically large rate increases in the United Kingdom during that time. In the United States, politics shifted to the left during the 1912 elections with pressures from Theodore Roosevelt's Bull Moose Party and from socialist Eugene Debs. These pressures were evident in the passage of the 16th amendment to the Constitution in 1913, which permitted the very income tax that was raised during World War I. Without this turn in progressive politics, higher tax rates during World War I would not have been possible. More generally, Mehrota suggests that the rise in progressivism set the groundwork for higher rates during the war and for a general ratchet up in rates over the years. With higher base level rates, perhaps it is easier to increase them further.

One century after World War I, could a rise in a new progressivism also set the stage for future attempts to tax the rich? With the rise of the superrich entrepreneurs—Musk, Zuckerberg, Bezos, Gates and many others—and the difficulties that the conventional income tax has in reaching their incomes, there has been an interest in new forms of taxation to address the gaps in our tax system. These proposals include wealth taxation starting for high-level millionaires and sophisticated strategies which would have the effect of taxing capital gains as they accrue, approaching the ideal Haig–Simons income base.

New Ideas for Taxing the Rich

New wealth taxes

In the run-up to the 2020 election, both Senators Elizabeth Warren and Bernie Sanders proposed wealth taxes. Warren's plan began with a 2 percent wealth tax on total net worth (assets minus liabilities) at the $50 million mark. Once wealth levels had crossed the $1 billion mark, the rate would rise to 3 percent. Sanders's proposal was more aggressive. He would begin taxing wealth of $32 million at 1 percent. Rates would then rise with wealth levels, reaching 5 percent for billionaires and then 8 percent for wealth holdings over $100 billion.

Both plans were projected to raise substantial sums of money. Warren's top rate of 3 percent would imply an extremely high implicit tax rate on income—if a portfolio of assets overall earned a 5 percent return, then a 3 percent wealth tax on those same assets would be equivalent to a 60 percent income tax rate (3/5 or 60 percent). Sanders's plan was meant to be confiscatory. With rates reaching as high as 8 percent, the goal was to reduce exceptionally large fortunes, along with raising money for the government. The rationale for this feature of the plan would be to diminish the outsized political influence of economic elites.

One might think that wealth taxation is inevitable as it perfectly meets the criteria set forth by Louisiana Senator Russell B. Long: "Don't tax you, don't tax me, tax the fellow behind the tree."[7] Warren emphasized that her wealth tax starting at $50 million would reach only the top 0.1 percent of taxpayers, so 99.9 percent would not be behind the tree. Despite its populist appeal, wealth taxes of the type envisioned by Warren and Sanders have not made political inroads in the United States.

There are several natural obstacles to wealth taxation. Those who are behind the tree are not a random 0.1 percent collection of Americans—they are the wealthiest Americans and have enormous political influence relative to their size. But aside from the pure political calculus, there are other issues standing in the way of wealth taxation. The European experience with wealth taxation was disappointing for progressives. Besides there is also the strong possibility that a wealth tax would run afoul of the U.S. Constitution and be struck down by the courts.

In 2018, the OECD published a report about wealth taxation. Its historical perspective was sobering:

> While 12 countries had net wealth taxes in 1990, there were only four OECD countries that still levied recurrent taxes on individuals' net wealth in 2017. Decisions to repeal net wealth taxes have often been justified by efficiency and administrative concerns and by the observation that net wealth taxes have frequently failed to meet their redistributive goals.[8]

In 2017 among the OECD countries, only Norway, Spain, Switzerland and France levied taxes on wealth. France, however, ended its net worth tax effective 2018 and replaced it with a tax on real estate. Only three wealth taxes remain today in the OECD countries.

There are several reasons why countries abandoned their wealth taxes. The taxes were complicated to administer and costly relative to the revenue they raised. They were unpopular, having been designed not for just the millionaires or billionaires but to reach more deeply down into the wealth distribution and to tax the merely affluent. Historically, tax evasion in Europe was common and relatively easy; as Gabriel Zucman documents, the wealthy found their way from Germany and France to Switzerland's financial hub.[9] Finally, within the European Union there were no state-induced barriers to mobility, so countries were limited in the types of taxes they imposed by fear of an exodus of the rich to other EU countries.

Proponents of a wealth taxation in the United States believed that they had answers to these difficulties. First, the thresholds for wealth taxation were set extremely high—$32 to $50 million—so that those being taxed were the truly wealthy, not just the merely affluent. Second, options for leaving the United States for other countries are not as easy as they are in Europe. Moreover, the United States in 2008 began to impose an exit tax for U.S. citizens, where expatriating citizens have their assets marked-to-market (i.e., valued at current market rates) and taxed on their capital appreciation. But even that might not be sufficient to deter a billionaire exodus, so the wealth tax proposals would have strengthened these exit taxes.

Finally, there are challenging administrative issues in implementing wealth taxation. While it is straightforward to find values for traded assets, there are difficulties with nontraded assets, such as with ownership interests in business enterprises that do not have marketable securities, artwork or unique real estate holdings. These items are all taxed at death for the wealthy under our current estate and gift tax regime, but only once at that time. Under a wealth tax, there would need to be annual valuations.

Estate tax disputes are often contentious. For example, the IRS claimed that Michael Jackson's name and likeness were worth $161 million at his death. His estate claimed they were only worth $2.1 million because of the decline of his reputation from accusations of child abuse. The Tax Court ruled in favor of the Jackson estate, valuing his name and likeness at $4.2 million.[10] Of course, people only die once, but reputations do rise and fall rapidly; valuing these changes yearly would be challenging for the IRS.

Proponents of wealth taxation argue that these cases are not typical and normal rules of thumb for valuation can be routinely used. After all, private equity firms routinely buy businesses with no marketable securities, calculating the value of the firm using a variety of different estimation techniques. Why should the IRS not be able to do this as well? Saez and Zucman also offered the following suggestion (perhaps tongue in cheek) for closely held businesses: if a wealth tax were 5 percent and a company thought the IRS valuation was excessive, it could simply surrender a 5 percent ownership interest of the company to the IRS.[11] Although this alternative would be unlikely to survive a legislative process, valuation issues are possible to address. One legal scholar asserted that "legal scholarship on valuation has devised a number of superior valuation methodologies based on formulaic prospective and retrospective methods."[12] While possible, such methods would require a concerted effort to justify them to the public and a continuing substantial investment in auditing resources.

The U.S. constitutional issues are complex and contested. The fourth clause of Article I, Section 9 of the U.S. Constitution—commonly known as the Direct Tax Clause—reads "No Capitation, or other direct Tax, Tax shall be laid, unless in Proportion to the Census or Enumeration herein before directed to be taken." What this means is that no head tax (capitation) or other "direct tax" can be levied by the Congress unless the revenues collected are in proportion to the population of the respective states. Direct taxes therefore must be apportioned by state populations. But what precisely are "direct taxes"?

This simple question had a profound effect on U.S. taxation. In 1895, the U.S. Supreme Court in *Pollock v. Farmers' Loan and Trust Co.* struck down an income tax that had been passed in the prior year because it concluded that taxing income derived from property was the equivalent of a direct tax. The United States did not resume taxing income until the passage of the 16th amendment in 1913. Legislation enacting an income tax quickly followed.

The 16th amendment authorized a tax on income, not on wealth. Would a tax on wealth be considered a direct tax and subject to apportionment? If so, revenues per capita from a wealth tax in Mississippi would have to be equal to those from New York. Since total net worth per capita in New York far exceeds the net worth per capita in Mississippi, tax rates on net worth would have to be vastly higher in Mississippi than in New York to comply with the constitutional requirement. This would make a wealth tax patently unfair. It would also make it largely ineffective, as it would limit the maximum tax rate that could be applied in the high net worth states and thus total potential revenue.

Constitutional and legal experts have actively debated the meaning of the Direct Tax Clause. Soon after the founding of the nation, the Congress enacted a direct tax on the ownership of carriages; in 1796, the Court ruled that this tax was not required to be apportioned as it would make little sense to do so and be contrary to sound public policy. As several scholars have argued, courts during the nineteenth century—until the Pollock case—were not inclined to expand the scope of direct taxation beyond land and capitation taxes (head taxes and taxes on enslaved persons).[13] The Pollock ruling then came as surprise. Despite the Pollock ruling, Congress instituted the first corporate tax in 1909, which was found constitutional because it was characterized as an excise tax for the privilege of doing business. Estate and gift taxes which clearly reach wealth also survived because they were also viewed as an excise or transfer tax, not a direct tax on wealth.

What would today's Supreme Court say on this matter? In 2012 in *NFIB v Sebelius*, the opinion upholding the Affordable Care Act, Chief Justice Roberts's opinion noted that the "narrow view of what a direct tax might be persisted for a century … In 1895, we expanded our interpretation to include taxes on personal property and income from personal property, in the course of striking down aspects of the federal income tax." By the narrow view, he meant direct taxes only meant taxes on land or poll taxes. The opinion went on to note, however, that in the *Eisner v. Macomber* tax case in 1919 "we continued to consider taxes on personal property to be direct taxes."[14] This dictum suggests that the Court could find a wealth tax that applied to property to be unconstitutional. For that reason, some supporters of wealth taxation have recommended backup provisions or other solutions to avoid constitutional scrutiny or to satisfy the apportionment requirement in novel ways.[15] But this would obviously make the legislative path for a wealth tax that much more complex.

Accrual Taxes

An alternative approach to reaching the fortunes of the very wealthy but without resorting to a wealth tax would be to revise the income tax to tax capital gains as they accrue. In 2019, Senator Ron Wyden of Oregon. Chairman of the Senate Finance Committee issued a proposal entitled "Treat Wealth Like Wages," which aimed to precisely do this.[16] The proposal received positive views from many tax policy experts as it had built on prior theoretical work by tax scholars.

Under Wyden's proposal, all tradable assets would be taxed annually at the rates applying to ordinary income (such as wages) on the increase in their value. Since values of tradable assets can be observed in the market, it would be straightforward to calculate their increase. For assets that were not traded, taxation would not occur until the assets were sold or gain otherwise realized, but there would be a look-back provision that would charge interest to account for the fact that taxes were not paid in the year in which the gain was accrued. Ideally, the interest charges would be such as to place the taxation of traded and nontraded assets on an equal footing. Transfers of assets, including gifts, would be considered a realization event which would trigger the look-back tax. Finally, these provisions would only apply to taxpayers with high levels of either income or wealth. Under the 2019 proposal, these provisions would be triggered if a taxpayer had income that exceeded $1 million for three consecutive years or $10 million dollars of assets for three years.

Wyden redesigned his plan during Congressional tax negotiations in 2021 but restricted it to extremely wealthy taxpayers. Under this version, the threshold to trigger the new taxes would be either $100 million in income for three consecutive years or $1 billion in wealth. Hence, the title of his proposed legislation—the "Billionaires Income Tax." According to an analysis provided by the Senator, it would apply only to 700 taxpayers yet raise billions of dollars in revenue.[17] After a flurry of interest, the proposal failed to advance into legislation.

Senator Wyden had cast his plan as an income tax partly to avoid potential constitutional issues that could plague the wealth tax. Although the consensus of most tax scholars is that taxing gains as the they accrue is less likely to run aground of constitutional objections compared to a wealth tax, there are some potential legal issues.

The first issue is whether realization is a constitutional requirement to impose an income tax. The 1919 Supreme Court case *Eisner v. Macomber* case first ruled that realization was required and the 1955 *Glenshaw Glass* case defined gross income in the tax code as an "undeniable accession to wealth, *clearly realized*, and over which the taxpayers have complete dominion."[18] (italics added) However, despite these cases, the Congress has enacted several laws imposing taxes on accrued gains. One example is the exit tax for expatriates discussed earlier in the chapter, although expatriation may be dubbed a realization event. But other taxes, including taxing imputed interest on discount bonds or taxes on the gains of certain futures market transactions which are not realization events, suggest that the realization requirement may not be that strict. Of course, a wholesale abandonment of the realization requirement as under the Billionaires Income Tax would be challenged in the courts and subject to legal risks.

The other potentially problematic feature of the Billionaires Income Tax concerns how the new system is phased in during the transition from the existing system. Once the tax is enacted into law, billionaire taxpayers would be required to pay all their accrued gains over five years, although they would also be eligible to deem up to $1 billion of tradable assets as nontraded and thereby only be taxed on that part of their wealth upon realization. But aside from that $1 billion, these accrued gains are likely to be a large component of wealth for many of the new billionaire class. For example, fortunes earned through IPOs and held as tradable stock would be subject to this tax. This looks suspiciously like a wealth tax, and a billionaire tax would rapidly bring the wealth tax arguments forward to the courts.

In President Biden's proposed budget for fiscal year 2023, the administration proposed another variant of a Wyden-style accrued income tax. For taxpayers with wealth holdings exceeding $100 million, there would be a new minimum tax of 20 percent that would apply to both realized and unrealized income. At its initiation, taxpayers would have up to nine years to pay past accrued gains. While this idea differs a bit from traditional wealth taxes and the Wyden accrued income tax, it would likely be subject to similar constitutional challenges.

Thus, taxing billionaires based on these new instruments—wealth taxes and accrued income taxes—may not be as straightforward as it seems. What about strengthening our existing estate and gift taxes, which have survived constitutional challenges over time?

Modernizing Estate and Gift Taxation

The estate and gift taxes are designed to tax transfers of wealth to future generations either on bequests upon death or through gifts. At its current level in 2023, the exemption level for an individual is $12.92 million or $25.84 million for a couple. At these high exemption levels, it has been estimated that fewer than 3,000 estates would have owed tax in 2021, less than 0.1 percent of estates.[19] Since 2010, the year that the estate tax rate temporarily went to zero, exemption levels have never fallen below $5 million per person or $10 million per couple. The current high level of exemptions would revert from the current levels to approximately $6 million per person in 2026 because of the phase outs built into the 2017 tax law. At this lower exemption level, the percentage of estates subject to the tax would increase to about 0.2 percent, still an exceedingly small percentage of all estates.

Despite the relatively small number of taxpayers directly affected by the estate tax, it has historically been an extremely unpopular tax. In my book, *Tax Fairness and Folk Justice*, I document the unpopularity of the tax and the strong movement to repeal it.[20] In that work, I offer a few psychological explanations for these beliefs.

The first psychological explanation is that the estate tax generates strong "moral mandates," which are nonnegotiable feelings that certain actions or policies are simply wrong. Under this category lies the strongly held belief that the tax is unfair because it taxes gains that have already been subject to the income tax. This double-tax argument shows up strongly in survey results. Another moral transgression is that the estate tax has been successfully framed as a tax levied not on rich estates but on death itself, which is associated with grief and family obligations. In tax historian Joseph Thorndike's words, "In that sense, the GOP's famous rebranding of the estate levy as a 'death tax' was brilliant."[21]

A second important psychological perspective is that the estate tax is viewed as a threat to the entire American way of life, which affects not only those subject to the tax but all Americans who feel part of the society and who aspire to become truly wealthy. Under this view, the estate tax is a system threat to the family and to American meritocracy. Americans have adopted positive stereotypes of wealthy people as valuable members of society and the estate tax directly targets them. This view is consistent with other accounts of the history of the estate tax. In their comprehensive review of the estate tax repeal movement, Michael Graetz and Ian Shapiro noted that tax policy debates are usually wars between justice and virtue. Here, justice generally comprises taxing those who can most afford it; virtue suggests that the state should reward an enterprising spirit and cultivate wealth accumulation rather than taking it away.[22] The average person, not likely to be subject to the tax, can still identify with a potential attack on American values. Indeed, according to some psychological accounts, precisely because they do not pay the tax, individuals may experience these feelings even more strongly.[23]

The impact of the estate tax is highly skewed to extremely high levels of wealth. According to the Congressional Budget Office, estates valued at $50 million or more accounted for 6 percent of all taxable estates in 2018 yet held 42 percent of assets reported by taxable estates in that year.[24] The extremely wealthy who are subject to the tax have the resources to carefully structure their estate plans to largely avoid paying significant tax. The CBO estimates that total tax revenues from the estate and gift tax in 2021 would be less than 0.1 percent of GDP.

With today's vast fortunes and a family exemption level of only $25 million, and a rate of 40 percent on transfers above that, there are strong incentives for the wealthy to find ways to circumvent the estate and gift tax. Consider a couple who wish to bequeath $125 million to their descendants. Without any estate planning, it would cost roughly $40 million to make such a transfer. Naturally, this creates great incentives for creativity in finding ways to avoid estate and gift taxation.

Indeed, we have seen remarkable examples of such creativity in recent years. Liberal reformers have sounded the alarms and warned about the proliferation of the so-called dynasty trusts, whereas vast sums of wealth can be passed from generation to generation with only minimal taxes. These groups have also provided an important public service by explaining how the ultrawealthy take advantage of current provisions in our estate and gift tax law.[25]

There are many different complex strategies to avoid transfer taxes, but here is an explanation of one important one to provide insights into how these strategies work—the grantor retained annuity trust or GRAT. Under a GRAT, the wealth holder (grantor) provides a major gift to a trust for its beneficiaries. At the same time, the trust is required to pay the grantor yearly annuity payments for several years based on a low government-set interest rate. The annuity payments are designed to be equal in value to the gift of assets to the trust—so no economic value has been exchanged. If the assets increase in value, all that appreciation accrues to the beneficiaries of the trust with no further taxes due. In a sense, the GRAT freezes the value of the contributed assets and allows further appreciation to go untaxed. If the assets fall in value, the GRAT fails and simply dissolves.

GRATs are thus perfect vehicles for contributing stocks that may appreciate over time, such as pre-IPO share holdings. Donors can create as many GRATs as they care to. According to reports, GRATs have been used by the late hotel magnate Sheldon Adelson, Facebook founder Mark Zuckerberg, JP Morgan Chase chair Jamie Dimon and Goldman Sachs former chair Lloyd Blankfein, and many others. GRATs are just one of many instruments the mega wealthy use to freeze valuations. Another important example is intentionally defective grantor trusts (IDGT) that can also accomplish similar ends.

Reformers have proposed legislation to restrict the use of these complex trust arrangements and make other reforms to the current estate and tax law. Because these strategies for the ultrawealthy are so complex and so much money is at stake, details of reform debates do not generally reach public consciousness. Lobbying pressure on Congress is intense and what appears to be a fix for a loophole one day will turn out to generate another loophole in the future. Perhaps crusading journalists and dedicated reformers can bring some of this to public attention and to have the Congress attend to some of weaknesses in current law. That said, the American public is ambivalent about the great fortunes of the new billionaires. As of October 2021, the eight wealthiest Americans, each with net worth exceeding $100 billion, were all first-generation wealth holders and not descendants of dynastic wealth themselves. Perhaps they also represent the American dream and could cause vigorous enforcement of taxes to be seen as an attack on the American way of life.

Ending Step-Up in Basis

Partly because of the complexity of many of the proposals for taxing the wealthy, the initial proposals from Biden Administration in 2021 were to end the step-up in basis at death and treat both death and gifts as realization events that would trigger capital gains taxes on appreciated assets– the tax basis of the asset would no longer increase (or step up) to its market value at the time of death. Gifts would need to be included otherwise donors could avoid the tax at death by making a gift while they were still living.

The administration recognized that they needed to make some initial concessions to have any chance of succeeding in the legislative process. The proposal only applied after a $1 million per person exemption, and family-owned businesses would not be subject to the tax until the business was no longer in the family. The current level of exemptions for owners of housing would still apply. For nonfinancial assets, there would be a fifteen-year period in which to pay the tax. Capital gains taxes paid at death or gift would be credited to any estate and gift tax obligation. Finally, the law would be prospective, effective only in the future for assets transferred at death or through gifts. Despite these concessions, the proposal did not make it through Congress. Groups purporting to represent small business led the opposition.

This was not the first time that there was an attempt to end the step-up in basis. In the Tax Reform Act of 1976, Congress enacted a carry-over basis provision at death. That meant that inheritors of property would not gain the step-up in basis, so if they inherited appreciated property and later sold it, they would pay taxes on their gain calculated relative to the basis of the property at the time they inherited the property. However, these rules were highly criticized and were repealed in 1980 without ever having gone into effect. A typical criticism of the rules was that it would often be impossible to determine the basis of property bought in the distant past. When the estate tax was temporarily repealed for 2010, the Congress had intended to institute a modified carry-over basis provision as well, but also retroactively repealed it.

Despite these failed attempts, tackling step-up in basis directly has its advantages over other alternatives. First, it deals directly with a weakness in the income tax. It is relatively easy to explain that these are taxes on gains that would otherwise escape taxation. Second, as the Biden administration proposal indicated, it is possible to build in some safeguards for family-owned businesses and situations where there may be short-run liquidity issues. Finally, it avoids our ambivalence with estate and gift taxes or transfer taxes generally. Nonetheless, any long-standing tax provision will seem to be normal and justified to people. It typically will also affect those with substantial means who will likely resent changes in long-standing practice.

As history seems to indicate, taxing the rich or near-rich is not easy and will take a politically opportune moment. Taxing extremely high income or extremely high wealth individuals has proven to be an elusive and difficult task, but there are some steps that can be taken if there is sufficient popular support for such taxes. Even with political will, such taxation must navigate conflicted popular sentiments and intricate legal and administrative issues.

Notes

1 Shaw and Stone, "Tax Data Show Richest 1 Percent Took a Hit in 2008, But Income Remained Highly Concentrated at The Top."
2 Piketty Saez, "Income Inequality in the United States, 1913-1998."
3 Piketty, *Capital in 21st Century*.
4 Auten and Splinter, "Income Inequality in the United States: Using Tax Data to Measure Long-term Trends."
5 Scheve and Stasavage, *Taxing the Rich*.
6 Mehrota, "Why Atlas Hasn't Shrugged: Review Essay."
7 While a similar sentiment had been expressed in the 1930s, this exact quote was from Russell Long in 1973. See Quote Investigator (Russell Long).
8 OECD Tax Policy Studies, "The Role and Design of Net Worth Taxes in the OECD," Executive Summary.
9 Zucman, *The Hidden Wealth of Nations*.
10 Sisario, "Michael Jackson's Estate is Winner in Tax Judge's Ruling."
11 Saez and Zucman, *The Triumph of Injustice*. Similar ideas have, at times, been offered for valuation for property tax purposes where taxpayers who dispute what they believe are excessive valuations by the government could offer their property up for auction at that price.
12 Gamage, "Five Key Research Findings on Wealth Taxation for the Super-Rich," 3–4.
13 Brooks and Gamage, "Taxation and the Constitution, Reconsidered."
14 National Federation of Independent Business v. Sebelius, 567 U.S. 519 (2012).
15 Brooks and Gamage, "Taxation and the Constitution, Reconsidered."
16 Wyden, Senate Finance Committee, "Treat Wealth Like Wages."
17 Wyden, Senate Finance Committee, "Billionaires Income Tax."

18 *Eisner v. Macomber* 252 US 189 (1920) and *Commissioner v. Glenshaw Glass Co.* 348 U.S. 426 (1955).

19 The CBO projects 2800 estates would be subject to the tax in 2021. CBO, "Understanding Federal Estate and Gift Taxes."

20 Sheffrin, *Tax Fairness and Folk Justice*, Chapters 4.

21 Thorndike, "The Not-So-Puzzling Unpopularity of the Estate Tax," 1081.

22 Graetz and Shapiro, *Death by a Thousand Cuts.*

23 This is based on system justification theory. See Sheffrin, *Tax Fairness and Folk Justice*, Chapter 4.

24 CBO, "Understanding Federal Estate and Gift Taxes."

25 Americans for Tax Fairness, "Dynasty Trusts."

Chapter 8

LOOKING BACK, LOOKING AHEAD

In this last chapter, I return to the basic theme of this book that underlying our tax controversies are a series of deeper and more fundamental issues. I first briefly review some of the underlying social, legal and economic factors that are below the surface and drive many of our tax controversies that we discussed in earlier chapters.

I then step back from our detailed investigations of ongoing controversies and look ahead to a few emerging issues about the tax system. First are questions of how we use the tax system for social ends and whether the tax system insures fiscal adequacy. How much can we rely on the tax system for other ends than raising revenue? Are we failing to raise sufficient funds through taxation to meet our ultimate financial obligations, while satisfying the apparent desires of the public?

Second, I explore a related topic revolving around taxation and democracy. What control should the public have over tax policy? Where does a country's national sovereignty begin and end? Should an international expert class determine the directions of national or international tax policy, or should the views and votes of the residents of the nation be the chief determinant of fiscal matters?

As we explored tax controversies in the preceding chapters, we saw that they were frequently driven by factors other than the distribution of the tax burden or "who got what." There are three broad categories of factors that lay beneath the surface of the controversies. The first is broadly social in nature and consists of a variety of sociological, psychological and philosophical perspectives on society. The second broad category is institutional and consists of legal and administrative issues pertaining to taxes. The third broad category is associated with the economics of taxation and the corresponding role of incentives.

Table 8.1 provides a summary of the themes that surfaced during our investigations cross-referenced by chapter and broken out into these three categories: Social, Legal/Administrative and Economic. In addition to providing a convenient summary of many of the key arguments in the book, this

Table 8.1 Underlying factors behind tax controversies

Chapter/Theme	Social	Legal/Administrative	Economic
What are Tax Policy Controversies About?	Justice and fairness (libertarian vs social perspectives). Procedural fairness in tax administration. Expressive theory of taxation (taxes convey social meaning). Corporate taxation or nontaxation.	Respect legal structures or fictions (e.g., corporations) while dealing with substance. Defining taxable income and the realization principle.	What is true economic income? How should corporations pay tax and where should they pay it?
The Rise and Fall of Classic Tax Reform	Sense of fairness that all income is taxed uniformly.	Limits on capital gains rates imposed by the "step up" in basis at death. Administrative and legal factors limit the reach of broad base taxation.	Excess burden and incidence of taxes. Tensions between broad base, uniform tax rates and excess burden. (e.g., charities, capital gains).
Should We Tax Income or Consumption?	Consumption tax perception issues. Is progressive wage taxation fair by itself? (Trust fund recipients) Are bequests or charity consumption? Worries about wealth accumulation. Perceptions of taxing borrowing or not taxing corporations.	Administrative issues in taxing durable goods and large financial transactions. Complications of taxing financial institutions. Complications with international taxation.	Wage taxes versus consumed income taxes and risky outcomes. How large are the true efficiencies from taxing consumption apart from taxing existing wealth?
Do We Need a New System to Tax Multinational Corporations?	Corporations not paying taxes but exploiting the market. Psychology of "entity taxation." Questions over corporate national identity.	Difficulties in implementing arm's length pricing rules for transfer pricing. Administrative issues in implementing worldwide OECD rules.	Efforts to reduce tax competition. Uncertain rationales for taxing corporations in a global economy.

(*Continued*)

Table 8.1 (Continued)

Chapter/Theme	Social	Legal/Administrative	Economic
Competing Perspectives on Tax Fairness	End-state versus rights-based theory of economic justice. Folk justice: equity theory, procedural justice, qualified perceptions of fairness. Intuitions of tax fairness based on desert and inherited or genetic advantages.	Administrative difficulties of taxing luck versus earned income or taxing windfalls.	Problems with implementing optimal tax theory (excess burden and redistribution). Super-star phenomenon and large fortunes.
Is the Tax System Racially Biased?	Interpreting disparate outcomes generally. Does racial tax accounting extend beyond expressive taxation?	Do the legal standards established for disparate impact contribute to the discourse on taxation?	Measurement issues for accounting for racial differences.
How Can We Tax the Very Wealthy?	Conflicted public views of taxing the wealthy and taxing gains at death.	Constitutionality of wealth taxes. Legal status of realization principle. Finding ways to tax gains in illiquid assets. Policing the estate and gift tax regime.	Measuring high-level incomes accurately. Economic advantages and disadvantages of private wealth accumulation.

table allows us to step back and reflect on the deeper influences on tax policy today.

Starting with the Social category, we see how tax policy is tied to deeper and often irreconcilable social perspectives. Taxes can be expressive, from deciding whether to legitimize taxing brothels to whether to interpret differential group outcomes through a racial lens. Taxes also reflect our fundamental beliefs about justice, but there are sharp differences in these views. Does justice consist of prescribed end-state patterns or, alternatively, of fair rules governing a competitive process? If it is the latter, are we comfortable with differences in wealth stemming from acquired or genetic advantages? From a moral perspective, when is uniformity in taxation required or when should legitimate distinctions among taxpayers matter? Should we judge relative well-being through how much people earn, or how much they consume? If so, are expenditures on charitable contributions or health care really consumption?

From the psychological side, our opinions on taxes will reflect our attitudes toward legal entities such as corporations. Should corporations be subject to tax, or should we look through them to the burdens placed on individuals? If we do tax corporations, does it matter if they are primarily domestic or foreign corporations—does that distinction even matter to the average person in today's world? In addition, our psychological predispositions toward death and future generations will be reflected in how we perceive the fairness and legitimacy of estate, gift and inheritance taxes.

The issues raised in the Legal/Administrative category have profound effects on the operation of the tax system. As we repeatedly encountered throughout the book, the realization requirement for income taxation sharply limits our ability to tax the very wealthy and prevents us from implementing an ideal Haig–Simons income tax. Whether this requirement is just a result of path dependence from prior legal decisions, or a constitutionally protected right is not a fully settled matter, nor are the potential U.S. constitutional limits on wealth taxation. Both the realization requirement and possible constitutional impediments to wealth taxation have played prominent roles in recent tax debates. But the realization requirement also has a practical administrative side. It is difficult to value complex assets—such as closely held corporations—until they are sold. Most of the recent proposals to tax the wealthy have had to make concessions to this fact and thereby make their proposals either too simple to be effective or too complex to be implemented.

Administrative issues also play a prominent role in the debate over the desirability of a traditional income tax versus a progressive, consumed income tax. Tax theorists have noted that taxing consumption rather than income could be much simpler, as there would no longer be a need for businesses to maintain detailed records for the depreciation of their investments or for individuals to keep track of the tax basis of their personal investments. But in moving from theory to practice, the same tax theorists recognized practical administrative problems in dealing with purchases of large durable goods—such as housing—or large financial commitments such as mortgage loans. These and other practical issues effectively forced advocates of consumption taxes into proposals for implementing them with a complex mixture of corporate and personal taxation. This method has its own limitations as well.

International taxation is another arena where administrative issues loom large. Administering a transfer pricing system to determine the income of separately incorporated entities operating within a single multinational enterprise but in multiple countries has proven to be extraordinarily complex. Its travails have generated political tensions throughout the world and have spawned increasingly complex proposals to develop alternative systems for multinational taxation, but the administrative foundations of these alternatives may be equally complex.

Finally, within the Economic category, basic economic principles shape the contours of tax policy in fundamental ways. How individuals and businesses respond to taxation limits the set of feasible policies. In particular, the concept of excess burden—the cost to the private sector of a tax beyond the revenue collected—dictates departures from purportedly ideal tax designs. If certain activities are very responsive to taxation, it is difficult to tax them at high rates. This fact partly underlies our lower rates of taxation for capital income. The optimal taxation literature in economics formalized our understanding of the tensions between using taxes for redistribution and the excess burden created through taxation.

Economic principles are also reflected in how we think about tax design. There are a host of examples. The pros and cons of traditional versus Roth IRAs are mirrored in the economic discussions of consumption versus wage taxation. On the international side, the economics of tax competition between countries and its linkages to tax avoidance strategies by corporations has been at the heart of recent international discussions. Even seemingly mundane tasks such as economic measurement have created controversies, such as whether the share of income accruing to the extraordinarily rich has really increased over recent years and what are the best methods to measure changes in incomes and tax burdens.

The diverse social, legal and economic perspectives make tax policy one of the more complex policy areas that directly affect wide-ranging constituencies. On the academic side, a diverse array of researchers—economists, legal scholars, accountants, psychologists, sociologists, philosophers and historians—have made major contributions to tax policy. Controversies sometimes reflect both intramural controversies within disciplines as well as alternative perspectives across disciplines. All these debates and viewpoints eventually filter into the public realm and affect public perceptions and political actors. Of course, distributional issues also come forward into the public debate. But the distributional issues are framed through the underlying social, legal and economic perspectives. It is no wonder that achieving any consensus on tax issues stretches the capabilities of any political system.

As we look ahead, the U.S. tax system will soon be pushed in other directions. The first is that we are simultaneously asking our tax system to do too much and not enough. By too much, I mean that the tax system at least in the United States has become the go-to institution to address our social concerns. We saw this in our discussion of tax expenditures in Chapter 2. The largest anti-poverty program in the United States is the earned income tax credit. While the EITC is a successful program, policing potential fraud in the system has absorbed valuable resources that could be more usefully employed in other areas. In recent years, however, we have further expanded the role of the tax system in administering expansions of child tax credits and economic impact payments during the COVID pandemic period. Both liberals and conservatives seem to gravitate to the tax code—liberals because they like the programs and seeming ease of administrations and conservatives both because they may not only like certain programs too (e.g., promoting pronatal policies with the child tax credit) but also see them through the lens of tax cuts.

The downsides to this trend are numerous. The Internal Revenue Service (IRS) cannot easily cope with these sustained expansions. While they were effective in distributing checks during the pandemic, the administrative, legal, staffing and technology issues that have emerged in recent years threaten timely resolution of its core business—collecting revenue to run the federal government. Failures to process returns, delayed refunds and the near impossibility of reaching a live agent to address tax questions are all emblematic of this failure. None of these difficulties have seemed to slow the spread of extraordinarily complex proposals to tax the wealthy or fundamentally redesign the international tax system—both of which would place major new burdens on the Treasury to write new rules and on the IRS to administer the system.

In the past, the courts gave the Treasury a bit of a break in writing rules and regulations for new legislation by allowing implicit exemptions from the normal administrative rules that governed other agencies when they issued regulations. But in recent years, the courts have begun to circumscribe this tax exceptionalism and have begun treating the Treasury like other agencies, subjecting it to the same provisos of administrative law that apply elsewhere in the federal government. The ultimate result of this trend will be not only a more deliberative approach to writing new rules and regulations, but also one that proceeds at a slower pace. This will make the process of adapting to fundamentally new legislation all that more complex for taxpayers.

The extra burdens on the Treasury and the IRS would not be as bad if the country were already collecting sufficient revenue to finance the government. Unfortunately, the United States is not on such a trajectory. Estimates from the Congressional Budget Office change over time but have consistently recognized an ever-growing debt to GDP ratio. Recent estimates project the government debt held by the public to reach 200 percent of GDP, far exceeding its maximum level of 100 percent of GDP during World War II and the pandemic.[1] Whether these levels of debt are sustainable without causing sharply rising interest rates and inflation are open questions and debated, but the consensus is that the gap between federal spending and revenue is putting the United States at great fiscal and economic risk.

There is no current consensus over what needs to be done. On the spending side, there is no appetite for rolling back Social Security or Medicare, and we have demonstrated little ability to control the long-term health costs that drive these trends. Political proponents of taxing the wealthy as discussed in Chapter 7 believe they can raise substantial revenue, but they have paired their plans with vast expansions of the welfare state—Medicare for All and expanded tax credits for families and children. No one wants to propose new and complex taxes just to reduce the deficit.

Income tax rates on both individuals and corporations could be increased but would require a much larger political faction in favor of high taxes than currently exists. In addition, the lessons of excess burden do not go away. With existing high state income taxes in large states like California and New York, there is little room in those places for federal tax increases. The size of our current fiscal gaps would persist even with plausible increases in income taxes and no further increases in spending.

This pessimism naturally leads to consideration of a supplemental value added tax (VAT) for the United States, as we are the only large high-income country in the world without a general consumption tax. The experience throughout the world is that this has been a robust method to raise sufficient revenue to fund programs both for the poor and middle class, offsetting its apparent regressivity, but severe obstacles remain to implement a U.S. VAT. A famous quote from Lawrence Summers highlights one major issue: "Liberals think it's regressive and conservatives think it's a money machine. If they reverse their positions, the VAT may happen."[2] Thinking of a VAT by itself, liberals do find it regressive, but the programs it could support could be very progressive. Thinking about it just as a tax is too narrow. Conservatives do worry that it would be too easy to raise VAT rates and grow the size of government. It is true that high VAT rates are associated with large governments throughout the world, but there is little evidence that the VAT was the cause of this growth.

Another major issue for the United States is that states have taken over the role of administering consumption taxes with their retail sales taxes. There are difficult and complex issues over how a federal VAT would interact with the states. Could a VAT coexist with existing state sales taxes? Could states convert their sales taxes to VATs and have this all administered federally? Canada has worked out complex arrangements along these lines, but it is far from clear that this could be adapted to the United States.

The fact that none of these alternatives looks desirable—unsustainable deficits, cutting popular social programs, raising income tax rates or implementing a VAT—does not mean the U.S. fiscal problem goes away. But it does suggest that we will need to move out of our existing tax and fiscal comfort zone in the not-too-distant future.

The second major challenge we face is to find the right balance of meeting fiscal challenges in a globalized world while also honoring popular sovereignty and ultimate democratic control of taxation. Every democratic society must find the right balance between designating experts to propose budgets and design tax systems that meet a nation's fiscal imperatives while also satisfying public demands for accountability, taxpayer protections (both from the state and from other citizens) and for policies that track public desires.

As Wolfgang Schön describes, societies use two complementary mechanisms to satisfy these often-conflicting demands by citizens. The first method consists of constitutional protections such as rules specifying uniformity of taxation, prohibitions against special tax concessions or limitations on tax rates or tax bases. The second method is control of taxation through direct voting or through representative bodies. Although individual countries may lean more on one mechanism than the other, these mechanisms are typically combined to provide both taxpayer input and taxpayer protection.[3]

In the United States, there are some constitutional constraints in specific areas. As we have discussed, the U.S. constitution may limit wealth taxation, and the Supreme Court has placed limits on states impeding interstate commerce through discriminatory taxes. State constitutions also may limit the types of taxes (e.g., prohibit local income taxes) or place limits on local property taxation. But in general, these constitutional provisions are the exception rather than the rule, and the Congress and state legislatures often have free reign to design tax laws.

On the other hand, citizens also face limits on their direct control of taxation. These limits are different at the local and national level. As noted, with respect to local government, communities are restricted by state laws in their ability to tax property or impose local sales or income taxes. Sometimes, as in the case of Proposition 13 in California, voters through direct democracy imposed these limits statewide. States themselves may also face limits imposed by the courts or by Congress.

At the national level, our system of checks and balances, as well as a tradition of federalism constrains the national government. Tax legislation must originate in the House of Representatives (the body closest to the people) but must also survive the procedural hurdles in the U.S. Senate. Lobbyists can sometimes push through legislation but are usually most effective in blocking legislation that would harm their interests. In recent years, major legislation that fundamentally changed the tax landscape—such as the 2017 Tax Cuts and Job Act—have only occurred when one political party had control of both houses of Congress and the presidency. Incremental changes, however, do occur even in the presence of divided government, sometimes through legislation and other times through regulations or court decisions.

This system, cumbersome as it may seem, does provide a type of stability— for example, the top personal tax rate since 1993 has only varied between 35 and 39.6 percent. But it also makes it difficult to envision the types of reforms that may be necessary to guarantee long-term solvency for the U.S. government. Corporate rates have fallen over this period from 35 percent to 21 percent, but this decrease can be attributed to international tax competition; the United States was a follower rather than a leader internationally in this trend.

One challenge to the current U.S. mix of constitutional constraints and representative democracy is the recent ascendency of international agreements into the politics of U.S. tax policy. President Biden's administration, in pursuit of its own domestic priorities, wholeheartedly embraced the OECD reform process and took a leading role in corralling international agreement to the Pillar 1 and 2 proposals. But they were far ahead of the Congress in signing onto these international arrangements. The details of these accords were developed and constantly refined by the staff of the OECD and not by Congress or its own staff.

The OECD bureaucracy operates out of the eye of the populace and often even the business community that will potentially be subject to new rules. In part because of this relative exclusion, the OECD staff can generate overly complex and potentially unresponsive rules that may satisfy a broad global constituency but not be responsive to major country concerns. The difficulty here is that a slight change in domestic political forces within influential countries—such as a change in the dominant parties in the United States—could derail a good deal of the OECD program and leave the state of the international tax system in chaos.

Regarding democracy and taxation, international organizations are subject neither to constitutional constraints nor to popular will expressed through democratic channels. This is a long-term recipe for fiscal confusion and dysfunction. We do not have a world government; trying to force international agreements through our carefully balanced domestic political fiscal system can be problematic.

What is missing from world government solutions to tax problems are precisely the nuances of tax policy that we have recounted in this book. Each country has its own perspective and history on social, legal and economic issues. These will need to be respected—otherwise, we may see the equivalent of political earthquakes that can arise by not paying close attention to the deeper factors that drive the politics of tax policy.

Notes

1 Congressional Budget Office, "The 2021 Long-Term Budget Outlook."
2 Gale and Harris, "Creating an American Value-Added Tax."
3 Schön, "Taxation and Democracy." Germany and other European countries in theory rely more on constitutional guarantees, while the United States is at the other pole with a stronger reliance on democratic control.

REFERENCES

Agersnap, Ole and Owen Zidar, "The Tax Elasticity of Capital Gains and Revenue Maximizing Rates." *American Economic Review: Insights* 3, no. 4 (2021): 300–416.

Alm, James, "Is the Haig-Simons Standard Dead? The Uneasy Case for a Comprehensive Income Tax." *National Tax Journal* 2 (June 2018): 370–8.

Alm, James, Stacy Dickert-Conlin, and Leslie Whittington, "Policy Watch: The Marriage Penalty." *Journal of Economic Perspectives* 13, no. 3 (1999): 193–204.

Altera v Commissioner, 9th Circuit Court of Appeals, 2019, https://law.justia.com/cases/federal/appellate-courts/ca9/16-70496/16-70496-2019-06-07.html

Altig, David, Alan Auerbach, Laurence Kotlikoff, Kent Smetters, and Jan Walliser, "Simulating Fundamental Tax Reform in the United States." *American Economic Review* 91, no. 3 (2001): 574–95.

Americans for Tax Fairness, "Dynasty Trusts: Giant Tax Loopholes that Supercharge Wealth Accumulation." February 2022, https://americansfortaxfairness.org/wp-content/uploads/DT-2.2.pdf

Arnold, Jens, Bert Brys, Christopher Heady, Åsa Johansson, Cyrille Schwellnus, and Laura Vartia, "Tax Policy for Economic Recovery and Growth." *Economic Journal* 121, Issue 550 (2011): F59–F80.

Atkinson, Anthony and Joseph Stiglitz, "The Design of Tax Structure: Direct versus Indirect Taxation." *Journal of Public Economics* 6, Issues 1–2 (1976): 55–75.

Atuahene, Bernadette and Christopher Berry, "Taxed Out: Illegal Property Tax Assessments and the Epidemic of Tax Foreclosures in Detroit." *UC Irvine Law Review* 9, no. 4 (2019): 847–46.

Auten, Gerald and David Splinter, "Income Inequality in the United States: Using Tax Data to Measure Long-term Trends." Unpublished, 2022, http://davidsplinter.com/AutenSplinter-Tax_Data_and_Inequality.pdf

Backman, Maurice, "Why Does Billionaire Warren Buffet Pay a Lower Tax Rate Than His Secretary?" *The Motley Fool*, September 25, 2020, https://www.fool.com/taxes/2020/09/25/why-does-billionaire-warren-buffett-pay-a-lower-ta/

Bakija, Jon, "Tax Policy and Philanthropy: A Primer on the Empirical Evidence for the United States and Its Implications." *Social Research* 80, no. 2 (Summer 2013): 557–84.

Bankman, Joseph and David Weisbach, "The Superiority of an Ideal Consumption Tax over an Ideal Income Tax." *Stanford Law Review* 58 (2006): 1413–56.

Batchelder, Lily L., "What Should Society Expect From Its Heir? The Case for a Comprehensive Inheritance Tax." *Tax Law Review* 63, (2009–10): 1–112.

Bearer-Friend, Jeremy, "Should the IRS Know Your Race? The Challenge of Colorblind Tax Data." *Tax Law Review* 73, no. 1 (2019): 1–68.

Birnbaum, Jeffrey, "Showdown at Gucci Gulch." *National Tax Journal* 40, no. 3 (1987): 357–61.

Birnbaum, Jeffrey and Alan Murray, *Showdown at Gucci Gulch*. New York: Vintage Books, 1988.

Bourguignon, Francois and Amedeo Spadaro, "Tax-Benefit Revealed Social Preferences." *Journal of Economic Inequality* 10 (2012): 75–108.

Bowman, Karlyn, "Public Opinion on Taxes, 1937 to Today." AEI Public Opinion Studies, American Enterprise Institute, April 2016.

Bradford, David, *Untangling the Income Tax*. Cambridge: Harvard University Press, 1986.

Brooks, John and David Gamage, "Taxation and the Constitution, Reconsidered." Forthcoming *Tax Law Review*, https://papers.ssrn.com/sol3/papers.cfm?abstract_id =4061257

Brown, Dorothy, *The Whiteness of Wealth: How the Tax System Impoverishes Black Americans and How We Can Fix It*. New York: Crown, 2021.

Chamley, Christophe, "Optimal Taxation of Capital Income in General Equilibrium with Infinite Lives." *Econometrica* 54, no. 3 (1986): 607–22.

Choi, Jung Hyun, "Breaking Down the Black-White Homeownership Gap." *Urban Institute*, February 2020, https://www.urban.org/urban-wire/breaking-down-black -white-homeownership-gap

Coase, Ronald, "The Nature of the Firm." *Economica* 4, no. 16 (1937): 386–405.

Commissioner v. Glenshaw Glass Co. 348 U.S. 426 (1955).

Congressional Budget Office, "The 2021 Long-Term Budget Outlook." Washington, D.C., March 4, 2021, https://www.cbo.gov/publication/56977

———, "The Distribution of Household Income, 2018." Washington, D.C., August 4, 2021, https://www.cbo.gov/publication/57404

———, "Understanding Federal Estate and Gift Taxes." Washington, D.C., June 9, 2021, https://www.cbo.gov/publication/57272

Cui, Wei, "The Digital Services Tax: A Conceptual Defense." *Tax Law Review* 73, no. 2 (2019): 69–111.

Dean, Steven A., "Filing While Black: The Casual Racism of the Tax Law." *Utah Law Review* 2022, no. 4 (2022).

Desai, Mihir, "Myths and Mysteries of the Corporate Income Tax." *Musgrave Lecture*, March 24, 2021 at https://www.cesifo.org/en/node/62081

Deveraux, Michael, Alan Auerbach, Michael Keen, Paul Oosterhuis, Wolfgang Schön, and John Vella, *Taxing Profit in a Global Economy*. Oxford: Oxford University Press. 2021.

Diamond, Peter and Emmanuel Saez, "The Case for a Progressive Tax: From Basic Research to Policy." *Journal of Economic Perspectives* 25, no. 4 (2011): 165–90.

Drenkard, Scott, "The Willis Commission Report: The Most Important Tax Study that You Probably Haven't Read." *Tax Foundation*, September 2, 2016, https:// taxfoundation.org/willis-commission-report-most-important-tax-study-you-probably -haven-t-read/

Dufresne, Louise, "Ronald Reagan's Testy Moment in the 1980 GOP Debate." *CBS News*, February 11, 2010, https://www.cbsnews.com/news/reagans-testy-moment-in -the-1980-gop-debate/

Dyreng, Scott and Michele Hanlon, "Tax Avoidance and Multinational Firm Behavior." In *Global Goliaths*, edited by C. Fritz Foley, James R. Hines Jr., and David Wessel, 361–436. Washington, D.C.: The Brookings Institution, 2021.

Eisenger, Jessie, Jeff Ernsthausen, and Paul Kiel, "The Secret IRS Files: Trove of Never-Before-Seen Records Reveal How the Wealthiest Avoid Income Tax." *Pro-Publica*, June 8, 2021, https://www.propublica.org/article/the-secret-irs-files-trove-of-never-before-seen-records-reveal-how-the-wealthiest-avoid-income-tax

Eisner v. Macomber 252 US 189 (1920).

Elliott, Justin, Patricia Callahan, and James Bandler, "Lord of the Roths: How Tech Mogul Peter Theil Turned a Retirement Account for the Middle Class Into a $5 Billion Tax-Free Piggy Bank." *ProPublica*, June 14, 2021, https://www.propublica.org/article/lord-of-the-roths-how-tech-mogul-peter-thiel-turned-a-retirement-account-for-the-middle-class-into-a-5-billion-dollar-tax-free-piggy-bank

Fehr, Ernst and Klaus M. Schmidt, "A Theory of Fairness, Competition, and Coordination." *The Quarterly Journal of Economics* 114, no. 3 (1989): 817–66.

Feinberg, Kenneth R., *Who Gets What*. New York: Public Affairs, 2012.

Fleurbaey, Mark and Francois Maniquet, "Optimal Income Tax Theory and Principles of Fairness." *Journal of Economic Literature* 56, no. 3 (2018): 1029–79.

Florack, Nicole and Steven M. Sheffrin, "Psychological Non-Equivalence of Tax Bases: An Empirical Investigation." *Proceedings of the 106th National Tax Association*, 2013, https://www.ntanet.org/conference/2013/11/106th-annual-conference-proceedings-2013/

Freeman, Samuel, "Original Position." In *The Stanford Encyclopedia of Philosophy* (Summer 2019 Edition), edited by Edward N. Zalta, https://plato.stanford.edu/archives/sum2019/entries/original-position.

Freiman, Christopher and Shaun Nichols, "Is Desert in the Details?" *Philosophy and Phenomenological Research*, 82, no. 1 (2011): 12–33.

Friedman, Milton, "Tax Reform Lets Politicians Look for New Donors." *Wall Street Journal*, July 7, 1986, https://miltonfriedman.hoover.org/internal/media/dispatcher/214375/full

——— "Why Tax Reform is Impossible." June 29, 2012, https://www.youtube.com/watch?v=TruCIPy79w8

Gale, William, "Public Finance and Racism." *National Tax Journal* 74, no. 4 (2021): 953–74.

——— and Benjamin Harris, "Creating an American Value-Added Tax." *Hamilton Project*, February 25, 2013, https://www.hamiltonproject.org/papers/creating_an_american_value-added_tax

Gamage, David, "Five Key Research Findings on Wealth Taxation for the Super-Rich." Unpublished, https://papers.ssrn.com/sol3/papers.cfm?abstract_id=3427827

Gates, Bill, "Why Inequality Matters." *Gates Notes*, October 13, 2014, https://www.gatesnotes.com/Books/Why-Inequality-Matters-Capital-in-21st-Century-Review

Graetz, Michael, "The Truth About Tax Reform." *University of Florida Law Review* 40, no. 4 (1988): 617–39.

——— and Ian Shapiro, *Death by a Thousand Cuts: The Fight Over Taxing Inherited Wealth*. Princeton: Princeton University Press, 2006.

Griggs vs. Duke Power Co. 401 U.S. 424 (1971).

Hall Robert E. and Alvin Rabushka, "A Proposal to Simplify Our Tax System." *Wall Street Journal* (December 10, 1981): 198.

———, *The Flat Tax*. Stanford: Hoover Institution Press, 1985.

Hemel, Daniel, "Beyond the Marriage Tax Trilemma." *Wake Forest Law Review* 54 (2019): 661–705.

Hettich, Walter and Stanley Winer, *Democratic Choice and Taxation*. New York and Cambridge: Cambridge University Press, 1999.

Hines, James R. Jr., "High Tax Heresy." Unpublished, November 2016, http://docplayer
.net/175511268-High-tax-heresy-james-r-hines-jr-university-of-michigan-and-nber
-november-2016.html

Institute for Taxation and Economic Policy, "55 Corporations Paid $0 in Federal Taxes
on 2020 Profits." April 2, 2021, https://itep.org/55-profitable-corporations-zero
-corporate-tax/

Internal Revenue Code, Section 482, https://www.law.cornell.edu/uscode/text/26/482

Isaac, Elliott, "Lecture Notes on Income Taxation." Available from author.

Judd, Kenneth, "Redistributive Taxes in a Simple Perfect Foresight Model." *Journal of Public Economics* 28, no. 1 (1985): 55–83.

Kaplan MCAT Prep, "Average Salaries for Doctors." January 3, 2022, https://www
.kaptest.com/study/mcat/doctor-salaries-by-specialty/

Kaplow, Louis, *The Theory of Taxation and Public Economics*. Princeton: Princeton University Press, 2008.

Kleinbard, Edward, "Stateless Income." *Florida Tax Review* 11, no. 9 (2011): 699–773.

Liebman, Jeffrey, "Who are Ineligible EITC Recipients?" *National Tax Journal* 53, no. 4. Part 2 (2000): 1165–85.

Mack, Eric, *Libertarianism*. Cambridge: Polity, 2018.

Mankiw, N. Gregory, "Spreading the Wealth Around: Reflections Inspired by Joe the Plumber." *Eastern Economic Journal* 36 (2010): 285–98.

—— and Matthew Weinzierl, "The Optimal Taxation of Height: A Case Study in Utilitarian Income Redistribution." *American Economic Journal: Economic Policy* 2, no. 1 (2010): 155–76.

——, Matthew Weinzierl, and Danny Yagan, "Optimal Taxation in Theory and Practice." *Journal of Economic Perspectives* 23, no. 4 (2009): 147–74.

McBride, William, "What is the Evidence on Taxes and Growth?" *Tax Foundation*, 2012, https://taxfoundation.org/what-evidence-taxes-and-growth/

McCaffery, Edward, *The Oxford Introductions to U.S. Law: Income Tax Law*. Oxford: Oxford University Press, 2012.

——, "A New Understanding of Tax." *Michigan Law Review* 103, no. 5 (2005): 809–938.

—— and James R. Hines, Jr., "The Last Best Hope for Progressivity in Tax." *University of Southern California Law Review* 83, no. 5 (2010): 1031–98.

McClelland, Robert, "A New Study Suggests Congress Could Raise Money By Increasing Capital Gains Rate to 47 Percent: But There is a Catch." *Tax Policy Center*, September 16, 2020, https://www.taxpolicycenter.org/taxvox/new-study-suggests-congress
-could-raise-money-increasing-capital-gains-tax-rates-47-percent

McIntosh, Kriston, Emily Moss, Ryun Nunn, and Jay Shambaugh, "Examining the Black-White Wealth Gap." *Brookings Institution*, February 27, 2020, https://www
.brookings.edu/blog/up-front/2020/02/27/examining-the-black-white-wealth-gap/

McLure, Charles E. Jr., and George R. Zodrow, "Treasury I and the Tax Reform Act of 1986: The Economics and Politics of Tax Reform." *Journal of Economic Perspectives* 1, no. 1 (1987): 37–58.

Meade, James, ed., *The Structure and Reform of Direct Taxation*, Institute for Fiscal Studies. London: George Allen and Unwin, 1978.

Mehrota, Ajay, "Why Atlas Hasn't Shrugged: Review Essay." *Florida Tax Review* 21, no. 2 (2018): 665–85.

Metcalf, Gilbert, "Consumption Taxation." In *Encyclopedia of Taxation and Tax Policy*, edited by Joseph Cordes, Robert Ebel, and Jane Gravelle, 74, Washington, D.C.: Urban Institute Press, 1999.

Miller, David, *Principles of Social Justice*, Cambridge: Harvard University Press, 1999.

Mirrlees, James, "An Exploration in the Theory of Optimal Income Taxation." *Review of Economic Studies* 38, no. 2 (1971): 175–208.

Moll, Benjamin, "Lecture 8. Positive Analysis in the Growth Model." *Princeton Lectures*, 2014, https://benjaminmoll.com/wp-content/uploads/2019/07/Lecture8_ECO503 .pdf

Moran, Beverly I. and William Whitford, "A Black Critique of the Internal Revenue Code." *Wisconsin Law Review* 751 (1996): 751–820.

Murphy, Liam and Thomas Nagel, *The Myth of Ownership*. Oxford: Oxford University Press, 2002.

Nam, Jeesoo, "Taxing Option Luck." *UC Irvine Law Review* 11, no. 4 (2021): 1067–118.

National Federation of Independent Business v. Sebelius, 567 U.S. 519 (2012).

Neubig, Thomas, "Disparate Racial Impact: Tax Expenditure Reform Needed." Council of Economic Policy, Policy Brief, March 2021.

Nordlinger v Hahn 505 U.S. 1 (1992).

Nozick, Robert, *Anarchy, State, and Utopia*. New York: Basic Books, 1974.

Orbitax The Tax Hub, "Israel Adopts Virtual PE Concept Based on a Significant Digital Presence." April 19, 2016, https://www.orbitax.com/news/archive.php/Israel-Adopts-Virtual-PE-Conce-19025

Organization for Economic Co-operation and Development, "Aligning Transfer Pricing Outcomes with Value Creation." Actions 8–10 Final Report, 2015, https://www.oecd.org/ctp/aligning-transfer-pricing-outcomes-with-value-creation-actions-8-10-2015 -final-reports-9789264241244-en.htm

———, BEPS ACTIONS, https://www.oecd.org/tax/beps/beps-actions/

———, Tax Policy Studies. "The Role and Design of Net Worth Taxes in the OECD." No. 26, 2018, https://www.oecd-ilibrary.org/taxation/the-role-and-design-of-net -wealth-taxes-in-the-oecd_9789264290303-en

O'Sullivan, Arthur M., Terri A. Sexton, and Steven M. Sheffrin, *Property Taxes and Tax Revolts: The Legacy of Proposition 13*, Cambridge: Cambridge University Press, 1995.

Oxoby, R. J. and J. Spraggon, "Mine and Yours: Property in Dictator Games." *Journal of Economic Behavior & Organization* 65, no. 3–4 (2008): 703–13.

Pechman, Joseph, ed., *What Should Be Taxed: Income or Expenditure?* Washington, D.C.: The Brookings Institution, 1980.

Pew Research Center, "Top tax frustrations for Americans." April 30, 2021, https:// www.pewresearch.org/fact-tank/2021/04/30/top-tax-frustrations-for-americans-the -feeling-that-some-corporations-wealthy-people-dont-pay-fair-share/

Piketty, Thomas and Emmanuel Saez, "Income Inequality in the United States, 1913– 1998." *The Quarterly Journal of Economics* 18, no. 1 (2003): 1–41.

Pomerleau, Kyle, "Understanding the Marriage Penalty and Bonus." *Tax Foundation*, April 23, 2015, https://taxfoundation.org/understanding-marriage-penalty-and -marriage-bonus/

Poterba, James, "The Recommendations of the President's Advisory Panel on Federal Tax Reform: A Two-Year Retrospective." *Proceedings of the 100th Annual Conference on Taxation, National Tax Association* (2008): 299–303.

President's Advisory Panel on Federal Tax Reform, *Simple, Fair and Pro-Growth*, November 2005, https://govinfo.library.unt.edu/taxreformpanel/final-report/ index.html

Quote Investigator (Russell Long). Available at: https://quoteinvestigator.com/2014/04 /04/tax-tree/. Accessed December 2022.

Raphael, Ray, "Debunking Tea Party Myths." *HISTORYNET,* April 1, 2010, https://www.historynet.com/debunking-boston-tea-party-myths.htm

Rawls, John, *The Theory of Justice.* Cambridge: Harvard University Press, 1971.

Reilly, Peter J., "Wandering Tax Pro Remembers the Tax Reform Act of 1986." *Forbes,* October 20, 2011, https://www.forbes.com/sites/peterjreilly/2011/10/20/wandering-tax-pro-remembers-the-tax-reform-act-of-1986/?sh=28052891fe0b

Richards, Kitty, "An Expressive Theory of Tax." *Cornell Journal of Law and Public Policy* 27, no. 2 (2017): 301–55.

Rosen, Harvey, "The Marriage Tax is Down But Not Out." *National Tax Journal* 40, no. 4 (1987): 567–75.

Rothstein, Richard, *The Color of Law: A Forgotten History of How Our Government Segregated America.* New York: Liveright Publishing, 2017.

Saez, Emmanuel and Stefanie Stantcheva, "Generalized Social Marginal Welfare Weights for Optimal Tax Theory." *American Economic Review* 106, no. 1 (2016): 24–45.

Saez, Emmanuel and Gabriel Zucman, *The Triumph of Injustice: How the Rich Dodge Taxes and How to Make Them Pay.* New York: W.W. Norton, 2019.

Sarkar, Shavak and Josh Rosenthal, "Exclusionary Taxation." *Harvard Civil Rights-Civil Liberties Review* 53 (2010): 620–80.

Scheve, Kenneth and David Stasavage, *Taxing the Rich.* Princeton: Princeton University Press, 2016.

Schön, Wolfgang, "Taxation and Democracy." *Tax Law Review* 72, no. 2 (2018–2019): 235–304.

Seicshnaydre, Stacy, "Disparate Impact and the Limits of Local Discretion After Inclusive Communities." *George Mason Law Review* 24 (2017): 663–701.

Shaviro, Daniel N., "Simplifying Assumptions: How Might the Politics of Consumption Tax Reform Affect (Impair) the End Product?" In *Fundamental Tax Reform: Issues, Choices, and Implications,* edited by John W. Diamond and George R. Zodrow. Cambridge: MIT Press, 2008.

Shaw, Hannah and Chad Stone, "Tax Data Show Richest 1 Percent Took A Hit In 2008, But Income Remained Highly Concentrated at The Top." Center of Budget and Policy Priorities, October 21, 2010.

Sheffrin, Steven M., "What Have We Done to the Corporate Tax System?" *Challenge* 25, no. 2 (1982): 46–52.

———, *The Making of Economic Policy.* Oxford and Boston: Basil Blackwell, 1989.

———, "Perception of Tax Fairness in the Crucible of Tax Policy." In *Tax Progressivity and Income Inequality,* edited by J. Slemrod, 309–32. Cambridge: Cambridge University Press, 1996.

———, *Tax Fairness and Folk Justice.* Cambridge: Cambridge University Press, 2013.

———, "What Role Can Desert Play in Designing Tax Policy?" *Pittsburgh Tax Review* 15, no. 1 (2017): 137–61.

——— and Rujun Zhao, "Public Perceptions of the Tax Avoidance of Corporations and the Wealthy." *Empirical Economics* 61 (2021): 259–77.

Shelley vs Kraemer 334 U.S. 1 (1948).

Sher, Itai, "Generalized Social Marginal Welfare Weights Imply Inconsistent Comparison of Tax Policy." 2022. Available at: https://sites.google.com/site/itaisher/research?pli=1. Accessed December 2022.

Singer, Natasha, "For Top Medical Students, An Attractive Field." *New York Times,* March 19, 2008, https://www.nytimes.com/2008/03/19/fashion/19beauty.html

Sisario, Ben, "Michael Jackson's Estate is Winner in Tax Judge's Ruling." *New York Times*, May 3, 2021, https://www.nytimes.com/2021/05/03/arts/music/michael-jacksons -estate.html

Special Committee on State Taxation of Interstate Commerce of the Committee of the Judiciary, House of Representatives, "State Taxation of Interstate Commerce." Washington, D.C.: Government Printing Office, 1964.

Straub, Ludwig and Ivan Werning, "Positive Long-Run Capital Taxation: Chamley-Judd Revisited." *American Economic Review* 110, no. 1 (2020): 86–119.

Syal, Rajeev, "Amazon, Google, and Starbucks Accused of Diverting UK Profits." *The Guardian*, November 12, 2012, https://www.theguardian.com/business/2012/nov/12 /amazon-google-starbucks-diverting-uk-profits

Sylvester, Melinda, "Congress should Not Raise Taxes on Black-Owned Business." *Saporta Report*, October 26, 2021, https://saportareport.com/congress-should-not-raise-taxes -on-investments-that-create-black-owned-business/columnists/david/

Tax Policy Center, "How Many People Pay the Estate Tax?" 2020, https://www .taxpolicycenter.org/briefing-book/how-many-people-pay-estate-tax

Tax Policy Center, "What are the Largest Tax Expenditures?" 2021, https://www .taxpolicycenter.org/briefing-book/what-are-largest-tax-expenditures

Thaler, Richard, "Anomalies: The Ultimatum Game." *Journal of Economic Perspectives* 2, no. 4 (1988): 195–206.

Texas Department of Housing and Community Affairs v. Inclusive Communities Project. 135 S. Ct. 2507 (2015).

Thorndike, Joseph, "Comment." In *Taxing Capital Income*, edited by Len Burman, Henry Aaron, and C. Eugene Steurele, 153–62. Washington, D.C.: Urban Institute Press, 2007.

———, "The Not-So-Puzzling Unpopularity of the Estate Tax." *Tax Notes*, March 7, 2016.

Tyler Tom R. and E. Allen Lind, "A Relational Model of Authority in Groups." *Advances in Experimental Social Psychology* 25 (1992): 115–91.

United States 9th Circuit Court of Appeals, *Amazon.Com & Subsidiaries v. the Commissioner of Internal Revenue 2019*, https://cdn.ca9.uscourts.gov/datastore/opinions/2019/08/16 /17-72922.pdf

United States Department of Treasury, *Blueprints for Basic Tax Reform*, 1977, https://home .treasury.gov/system/files/131/Report-Blueprints-1977.pdf

———, *Tax Reform for Fairness, Simplicity, and Economic Growth*, 1984.

———, "Advancing Equity Analysis in Tax Policy." *News Release*, December 14, 2021, https://home.treasury.gov/news/featured-stories/advancing-equity-analysis-in-tax -policy

———, Tax Expenditures. Fiscal Year 2023, https://home.treasury.gov/policy-issues/ tax-policy/tax-expenditures

United States Department of Treasury Regulations Allocations of Income and Deductions Among Taxpayers. 26 CFR 1.482-1 (b)(1).

United States Senate, Permanent Subcommittee on Investigations, "Caterpillar's Offshore Tax Strategy." April 2014, https://www.hsgac.senate.gov/subcommittees/ investigations/hearings/caterpillars-offshore-tax-strategy

United States Senate Committee on Finance, "Tax Talk: The $2+ Trillion Lockout." July 26, 2017, https://www.finance.senate.gov/chairmans-news/tax-talk-the-2-trillion -lockout

Warren, Elizabeth, "You Didn't Build That" Speech. Elizabeth Warren Wiki, https://elizabethwarrenwiki.org/factory-owner-speech/

Washington v. Davis 426 U.S. 229 (1976).

Weiner, Juli, "The Rise of Romney's 'You Didn't Build This' Meme." *Vanity Fair*, July 18, 2012, https://www.vanityfair.com/news/2012/07/The-Rise-of-Romneys-You-Didnt -Build-That-Meme

Weinzierl, Mathew, "Revisiting the Classical View of Benefit-Based Taxation." *Economic Journal* 128, Issue 612 (July 2018): F37–64.

———, "The Promise of Positive Optimal Taxation: Normative Diversity and a Role for Equal Sacrifice." *Journal of Public Economics* 118 (2014): 128–42.

Welch v. Helvering. 290 U.S. 111.

Williams, Roberton C., "Taxing Millionaires, Obama's Buffet Rule." April 11, 2013, https://www.taxpolicycenter.org/taxvox/taxing-millionaires-obamas-buffett-rule

Wintour, Patrick, "Boris Johnson among Record Numbers to Renounce American Citizenship in 2016." *The Guardian*, February 9, 2017, https://www.theguardian.com/politics/2017/feb/08/boris-johnson-renounces-us-citizenship-record-2016-uk-foreign -secretary

Wyden, Ron, Senate Finance Committee, "Treat Wealth Like Wages." September 12, 2019, https://www.finance.senate.gov/imo/media/doc/Treat%20Wealth%20Like %20Wages%20RM%20Wyden.pdf

———, "Billionaires Income Tax." October 27, 2021, https://www.finance.senate.gov/imo/media/doc/Billionaires%20Income%20Tax%20-%20One%20Pager.pdf

INDEX

Note: Page numbers in bold refer to tables.